MANCHESTER'S MILITARY LEGACY

STEVEN DICKENS

Pen & Sword

MILITARY

To the memory of Private Charles Henry Dickens (No. 15405) of the 8th Battalion King's Own (Royal Lancaster Regiment), who died on 16 August 1916, aged twenty-eight, during an assault on Lonely Trench, at 17:40 hours, located just to the north of Fricourt. This was part of the campaign historically known as the Battle of the Somme.

Dulce et decorum est pro patria mori.

First published in Great Britain in 2017 by
PEN AND SWORD MILITARY
an imprint of
Pen and Sword Books Ltd
47 Church Street
Barnsley
South Yorkshire S70 2AS

Copyright © Steven Dickens, 2017

ISBN 978 1 52670 778 9

Typeset by Aura Technology and Software Services, India
Printed and bound in Malta by Gutenberg

Pen & Sword Books Ltd incorporates the imprints of Pen & Sword
Archaeology, Atlas, Aviation, Battleground, Discovery, Family History, History, Maritime, Military, Naval,
Politics, Railways, Select, Social History, Transport, True Crime, Claymore Press, Frontline Books, Leo
Cooper, Praetorian Press, Remember When, Seaforth Publishing and Wharncliffe.

For a complete list of Pen and Sword titles please contact
Pen and Sword Books Limited
47 Church Street, Barnsley, South Yorkshire, S70 2AS, England
email: enquiries@pen-and-sword.co.uk
website: www.pen-and-sword.co.uk

CONTENTS

The Royal Regiment of Fusiliers exercising their Freedom of the City in Rochdale, Greater Manchester, 2009. (Photo Adam Kerfoot-Roberts)

INTRODUCTION

Manchester's Military Legacy focuses on five major military events in the history of Manchester that have left the city with a lasting legacy into the twenty-first century. A legacy is something that is handed down, or remains, from a previous generation or time, so unfortunately it has not been possible to include every military influence on the city, although those not included remain important in their own right.

The book begins with the Roman invasion of Britain and the establishment of the Roman fort of Mamucium in AD 79. The development of a defensive stronghold close to the confluence of the rivers Irk and Irwell, built to guard the Roman road between Chester (Deva Victrix) and York (Eboracum), led to the growth of a surrounding *vicus* (settlement) and the economic development that went with it. The fort at Castlefield remains as a monument to Manchester's origins.

The English Civil War and the Siege of Manchester in 1642 influenced Manchester's political destiny. Manchester supported the Parliamentarian cause in the war and as a result its long-term legacy was to see it without Parliamentary representation until the Reform Act of 1832. The Victorian statue of Oliver Cromwell, presented to the city and situated outside Manchester Cathedral, remained a contentious issue until its removal to Wythenshawe Park.

The Peterloo Massacre of 1819 also had a profound influence on the development of liberal politics in Manchester, as well as parliamentary reform in the United Kingdom. The massacre of protesters for political reform at St Peter's Fields when their demands consisted of universal suffrage and reform of the House of Commons, is commemorated in a red plaque on the former Free Trade Hall, close to the site of the massacre by charging cavalry.

The Manchester Regiment played an important part in the Boer War (1899–1902) and the global conflicts of the First World War (1914–18) and the Second World War (1939–45). Carrying Manchester's name into battle across foreign fields, the Manchester Regiment raised 'Pals' battalions of local men, who conducted themselves with honour and bravery, and whose city commemorate their sacrifices on the cenotaphs and memorials given prominence throughout Manchester.

The Manchester Blitz of December 1940 devastated the city centre and had long-term consequences due to the destruction of its infrastructure. The bravery and resolve of its citizens helped to preserve Manchester's proud position against a determined enemy. After the end of the war the city rose from the ashes of conflict to become the vibrant, cosmopolitan city we see in the twenty-first century. Despite recent attempts to dent that resolve, through the tragedy of the Manchester Arena bomb, the city has again displayed the same bravery that saw its communities through the blitz. One thing is for certain: Manchester united will continue to thrive for all its citizens.

1. THE ROMAN FORT OF MAMUCIUM C. AD 79 TO C. AD 411, AND ITS LEGACY FOR THE DEVELOPMENT OF MODERN MANCHESTER

'It is not every great city that is able – by merely peeling off the accumulation of centuries – to expose to view under the very shadow of its railway viaducts and amid the roar of its traffic the relics of a vanished Empire, to lay bare the very streets trodden by men who may have been present at its own beginnings and to pick up objects left there by them nearly two millenniums ago.'

F. A. Bruton, *The Roman Fort at Manchester*

The modern site of the fort (foreground), looking south-west towards the railway viaducts at Castlefield.

The modern city of Manchester owes its foundation to the Roman invasion of Britain. Their 'acculturation' of the Brigantes territory to become a province of the Roman Empire, as Agricola advanced on into Scotland, led to the establishment of a Roman fort at Mamucium around c. AD 79, probably initially built upon the site of the ancient Britons' defensive hill fort. Eventually, a larger fort was established, around c. AD 160 and then c. AD 200, as the size of the garrison was increased. Then a settlement, or *vicus*, on the west, north and east sides of the fort, originating from the late first and early second centuries, grew outside the boundary walls of the fort in order to service its requirements. These requirements included extensive metalworking, presumably for the repair and production of weaponry and protective armour for the forts of the West Pennines, as well as domestic items: the provision of slaves for domestic use, the provision of homes for the families of soldiers, and the site of markets and domicile of merchants, needed to service the needs of the auxiliaries resident at the fort. This is the first definite record of Roman settlement in Manchester, dating from around c. AD 79 and lasting until the Romans left, around c. AD 410, after which the *vicus* declined and was eventually abandoned. This chapter will seek to understand what influence the military occupation of Manchester by the Romans had on its long-term development and what survives today in terms of the Romans' military legacy, with the focus firmly on the fort at Castlefield as a permanent memorial to their occupation.

The site of the fort (foreground), and the Granaries beyond, as seen from Northgate.

The Roman Campaign against the Brigantes and Segantii

What of the native peoples who were encountered by the Romans on their invasion of the north-west of England, and who survived to form a new society after the Roman withdrawal? Charles Roeder in his book *Roman Manchester* (1900 pp. 59-116) provides us with some interesting information about what the Romans could expect on their arrival in the north-west of England from its native inhabitants.

The west coast, from the River Mersey to the River Lune, was occupied by the Segantii and towards the slopes of the Pennine chain in the east, between the hills of Manchester, Leeds and Sheffield, by the south-western Brigantes. The Segantii dominated the estuary regions of the Ribble, Wyre and Lune, which afforded them great security and meant that the Roman advance found it difficult to dislodge or attack them. General Gnaeus Julius Agricola (Agricola) had to advance through the region in a pincer movement, from both the land and sea simultaneously. The Segantii centre of power was towards Walton and Ribchester, which were assimilated by Agricola and successive generals into a fort and stronghold. Its strategic aim was defensive, with the purpose of intercepting any localized uprising before it had the opportunity to develop into something which threatened regional security.

The Brigantes occupied the entire length of the Pennine chain and its slopes from the Solway Firth to South Yorkshire and consisted of several clans. According to Roeder they

Charles Roeder (1848–1911) was a native of Gera, in the province of Thuringia, Germany. He came to Manchester in 1869, aged twenty-one, to engage in commerce, devoting his spare time to research in languages, geology, botany, history and antiquities. His obituary in the *Manchester City News* of 16 September 1911 states,

The settlements of the Romans in the district had a peculiar fascination for him. He saw the effect that dominant conquest had in planting a civilised stronghold where now stands Manchester, one of the greatest cities in the world. It had, however, no classic records beyond that of its Latin name, and except in one or two instances, objects relating to that period, which had been discovered from time to time, had been dispersed as more curios and lost. Manchester in this respect had been peculiarly unfortunate, and Charles Roeder sought with keen eagerness to remedy the fault. For many years he patiently watched casual excavation, and was quick to distinguish fragments of Roman pottery and other objects when flung out with earth and clay by the spade. These antiquities have now been acquired for the city by the 'Old Manchester and Salford Committee,' and may be seen in the Roeder Collection at the Old Manchester and Salford Exhibition at Queen's Park. His observations on local Roman matters are on record in the transactions of the Lancashire and Cheshire Antiquarian Society, and are pioneer work in that direction. He became a member of that society in 1887, and was elected an honorary member in 1904.

were a 'fierce and dauntless race of fighting men and gave no little trouble to the Romans, who found them a strong, rebellious and restless nation'. (p. 62) The southern reaches of their territory were the more important ones, which was reflected in the distribution of Roman forts, roads and settlements across the region. The Roman road from the eastern gate of Mamucium, which ran through modern-day Newton Heath and Hollinwood to the Roman fort and fortlet at Castleshaw and then on to Slack and that from Hunts Bank, via Long Millgate, Castleton, Rochdale, Littleborough, Blackstone Edge, to Sowerby Bridge, ran straight through the Brigantes territory. The Brigantes also dominated the Pennines' western slopes and the foothills, which ran and spread out towards the fort at Mamucium. Before the Roman occupation this natural defensive stronghold, on a sandstone ridge overlooking the confluence of the rivers Medlock and Irwell, would have been occupied by a clan of the south-western Brigantes according to Roeder. The courses of the rivers Irk, Medlock, Mersey, Irwell, Roche and Tame would also have settlements of Brigantes scattered along them. Here the native Britons were Brythonic Brigantes, probably heavily reliant upon the river system for their survival. The Segantii were based further north along the west coast of Lancashire, around the Fylde, and separated from the Brigantes by

Site of the Roman fort, looking east, showing the modern landscaping (foreground) and Northgate beyond. The Beetham (or Hilton) Tower (centre) is at Deansgate.

some difficult to traverse terrain, including forests, swamps and mosses. To the south of the Brigantes were the Cornavii, along the southern banks of the River Mersey. This was the situation upon the arrival of the Roman armies in the region.

Roman campaigning against the indigenous British tribes tended to follow a distinct and disciplined pattern, helping Agricola to consolidate the Roman advance into the north of England and push on into Scotland. However, the Brigantes were formidable enemies and although the Roman armies were a very effective attacking force, they were much less efficient at dealing with 'guerrilla warfare' over the sort of mountainous terrain they were likely to encounter in the Pennines.

Quintus Petillius Cerealis was probably born in Umbria, Italy, c. AD 29. A Roman general and son-in-law of the emperor Vespasian, he suppressed the Batavian Revolt in AD 70. Little is known of his early career, but we do know that he was the commander of the Ninth Legion Hispana in AD 60. This unit was stationed in two camps at Longthorpe and Newton-on-Trent, but unfortunately suffered some heavy losses, totalling around a third of its strength, during the revolt of Queen Boudicca. Cerealis did not reach the next stage of the usual sequence of offices, which would imply that he was held responsible for the rout of his unit. However, in AD 70 Vespasian rewarded Cerealis for his role in the civil war. Vespasian sent a large expeditionary force across the Alps to subdue the Batavian Revolt, commanded by Cerealis. It was one of the largest armies any Roman general had commanded. Later that year Cerealis went to

Britain, where he commanded three legions (II Adiutrix) in a war in southern Scotland. He was appointed Governor of Britain in AD 71, being supported by Agricola, the commander of the XX Valeria Victrix. Cerealis used York as his base in this campaign and also campaigned against the Brigantes of northern England. On his return to Rome he was made a suffect consul, in AD 74, and was then awarded a rare second consulship in AD 83.

Quintus Petillius Cerealis.

The legions under the governorship of Quintus Petillius Cerealis (Cerealis), or Agricola, would also have encountered resistance from the Brigantian hill and mountain tribes in their fortified stronghold at Mamucium. Therefore, units of Roman auxiliaries were often used to garrison strategic sites such as river crossings and Pennine valleys, whilst the elite legions were kept in reserve at Chester and York in case they were needed to engage a more resolute enemy over a wider area. There were many basic tactics that the Roman armies used in order to engage their enemy; however, any military manuals used by the Romans to train their armies do not survive as primary sources. We are reliant upon the work of historian Publius Flavius Vegetius Renatus, dating from the late fourth century. The *De Re Militari*, *Epitoma Rei Militaris*, or *Rei Militaris Instituta*, incorporates parts of the work of Sextus Julius Frontinus (c. AD 40–c. AD 103) and gives us insight into the Roman military system, its practices, principles and mentality. Frontinus was governor of Britain from c. AD 73 to c. AD 77, subjugating the Silures of south Wales and is believed to have campaigned against the Brigantes. He was succeeded by Agricola, the father-in-law of historian Tacitus.

Vegetius emphasized the training of recruits, the study of military strategy, the maintenance of supply lines and logistics during a campaign, professional leadership and the use of tactics adaptable and relevant to a specific enemy. His influence on military

Castlefield Basin, looking north-west.

Castlefield Basin, looking south-west.

strategy lasted into the nineteenth century. Vegetius lived in the fourth and early fifth centuries and his original work has undergone several revisions since. It is now based on the Roman armies of the mid-to-late Republic. However, his work represents the closest written record we have of the way the Roman military conducted itself in battle situations and probably represents the ideal scenario, taken from the example of the early Roman Empire.

The Roman Empire's army at Mamucium initially consisted of one cohort of auxiliaries at the garrison. It is not known which unit held the fort, but it is likely that its infantry came from one of the north-western provinces of the Roman Empire. Inscriptions have been found indicating that soldiers from modern-day Portugal, Spain, Switzerland and Austria served at Manchester and at nearby garrisons like Melandra and Slack. For some of these soldiers who originated from countries with a more Mediterranean climate it must have been hard going. As a former project assistant at Castleshaw Roman fort in 1986–87, I witnessed some particularly harsh winter days on Castleshaw Moor. The Roman auxiliaries must have wondered what they had let themselves in for! The auxiliaries were recruited from amongst native peoples who had been incorporated into the Roman Empire after their conquest and assimilation. They were to serve in the Roman

Flavius Vegetius Renatus was a patrician and reformer with very little military experience. He lived in an era when cavalry and foreign auxiliary levies had undermined the traditional Legionary formation. This was initially based on a disciplined infantry and cohesive administration, which had become corrupt and inefficient. His treatise, *Rei Militaris Instituta*, was written sometime between c. AD 384–c. AD 389 and advocated a revival of the old system based on the values of the early Roman Empire. However, the increasingly ineffective armed forces of the later Roman Empire took little heed of the work of Vegetius and it was not until the Middle Ages that he began to gain recognition in military circles. In particular, his writings on siege-craft and on the need for discipline were studied and continued to be influential until the nineteenth century. This was, in part, due to the fact that Vegetius was the first Christian Roman to write on military affairs.

army for twenty-five years. Upon completion of their full term as auxiliaries they were then granted Roman citizenship, which also included any wives and children. This meant that they had rights and privileges granted in Roman law not enjoyed by native peoples. The men from the Manchester garrison in all probability settled in the *vicus*, outside the boundaries of the fort, with their wives and children on their retirement.

The armour and equipment of an auxiliary infantryman in the first century AD was inferior to that of the Legionary. He had a light shield, which was flat and oval. This meant that there were no corners to snag, making it better suited for individual combat, in loose formation and over difficult terrain, such as that encountered in the Pennines. His equipment was better suited to a light, mobile fighter rather than to the disciplined Legionary on the battlefield. Therefore, it is not hard to imagine an auxiliary patrol, in defence of say a river crossing, encountering and repulsing effectively a Brigantian surprise attack. Instead of a *pilum*, the throwing spear of the Roman Legionary, an auxiliary soldier would carry the *hasta*, a more basic stabbing spear better suited to close-quarter combat. For tactical formations we can refer to Vegetius's writings for an idea of the type used by an auxiliary soldier. In situations such as a surprise attack on uneven ground an auxiliary patrol would, in all probability, adopt a 'skirmishing formation'. This was a widely spaced line-up of soldiers and not the typical tightly packed ranks of Legionary units more suited to the battlefield. Every second soldier would step forward a few paces, thus increasing the width of the front line, with the gaps created covered by the second line of soldiers. The wide spaces created between each soldier thus allowed the individual fighter greater mobility and made an advance over uneven terrain much quicker and easier. Equally, it could also allow for a swift withdrawal of units through a formation.

The Roman armies were likely to have first encountered the Britons in fortified possession of Castlefield, which was partly built at a level of roughly 105 feet towards the south-west on a rocky, red-sandstone ridge within the angle of two low-banked

The Great Northern Railway Goods Yard under construction at Deansgate, looking towards Castlefield, in 1898.

confluent rivers. This was the type of defensive site that could be easily adapted and was generally preferred by the Romans for the erection of their camps. Brigantes would also, in all probability, be lying in ambush around the environs of Hunt's Bank, from where they were driven away, and the encampment immediately occupied and adapted for Roman use. These remains now lie beneath the site of Manchester Cathedral and Chetham's College. The Romans eventually moved their site to the larger fortified area that we see at Castlefield today, more suited to their militaristic purposes. Roeder (p. 115) believes that the native Brigantes were later allowed to return, while the new *castrum* at the River Medlock assumed a military identity. At this time what we now know as Deansgate, one of Manchester's main shopping and entertainment districts, would have been at the centre of Roman life. It was occupied by soldiers, traders and officials, while the Brigantes would have gravitated towards their ancient stronghold on the banks of the River Irk. This meant that in the course of time Roeder believes the settlement would have witnessed the polarization of its ancient populations, with the Brito-Roman (Brigantian) upper hill town and the Romans based at their lower site at Castlefield. We know from later excavations that a *vicus*, a settlement outside the walls of the Roman fort, developed and grew in order to serve it economically, which

Deansgate, looking towards the junction of Quay Street (left) and Peter Street (right). Note how straight this section of Roman road is.

ultimately also led to social interaction and a more 'fluid' society, with Romans forming relationships and producing children. Thus, Roeder (p. 116) reminds us that Mamucium meant 'mother stone edge', the original site of the Britons and the older Roman site, while the newer site at Castlefield was named Manucium. Another translation of Mamucium was 'breast-like hill', reminding us of the reasons why this location was chosen as a defensive stronghold.

However, on the withdrawal of the Roman army from Britain the fort at Manchester did not go into an immediate decline. 'We have no palpable evidence, as at Ribchester, of the fate of the station on the "departure" of the Romans about 411; I particularly searched for charred wood work and other proofs of destruction or conflagration, but found nothing pointing to such a catastrophe. The latest coins discovered refer to Anastasius I 491–518; close to the Ribchester road, at Higher Broughton, which clearly shows that the stations cannot have been entirely deserted or abandoned, but must have existed long after Ribchester, which, being more exposed and within easier reach of Picts and Scots and other marauders, was apparently already sacked or even destroyed.' There is also reference to Roman shield bosses possibly dating to the fifth century, as further proof of a more gradual decline in Roman influence. (Roeder p. 56)

This photograph shows the steep incline from Castlefield Basin, as seen from the fort's defensive wall in front of the Granary. Note the defensive ditch (right foreground) in front of the wall.

Roman Development of Castlefield, c. AD 79–c. AD 410

The Romans believed that it was their destiny to rule the known world. This was to be achieved by the Roman army, one of the most efficient fighting forces in the ancient world, and an associated system of government which emphasized military success. The Roman career politician had to achieve success on the battlefield in order to hold the highest offices of state – hence the might and brutal determination of the Roman military machine to establish the Roman Empire. Early Manchester, with its frontier fort and associated civilian settlement, is a type of site found throughout the fringes of the Roman Empire. Roman forts and their *vici* are to be found in such diverse countries as Germany, Turkey, Russia and Libya.

The Roman fort of Mamucium was established c. AD 79 on a sandstone ridge overlooking a nearby crossing on the banks of the River Medlock. It was constructed of timber, with earthen ramparts and a double-ditch, and was the base for a cohort of auxiliary infantry (around 480–500 men). The fort was constructed as part of the complex of fortifications erected during the campaigns of General Agricola against the Brigantes. It guarded the crossing of the strategic road from York (Eboracum) to Chester (Deva Victrix) with that of a road running from the Fosse Way to the north.

The fort's defensive ditch system, as seen from Northgate and looking towards the Vicus and Liverpool Road.

General Gnaeus Julius Agricola (AD 40–AD 93) was a Roman statesman and Governor of Britain who conquered large areas of northern England, Scotland and Wales. His son-in-law was the historian Tacitus, who wrote a detailed biography of Agricola, which has survived into the modern era. Agricola was born in southern France into a high-ranking family and began his career as a military Tribune in Britain. During the civil war of AD 69, Agricola supported Vespasian, who became emperor and appointed Agricola to command a Roman legion in Britain. He then served as Governor of Aquitania (south-east France) for three years before returning to Rome. In AD 78 he was made Governor of Britain and began a campaign in north Wales, crossing the Menai Straits to take Anglesey. In AD 79–80 he consolidated Roman military power in Scotland, building forts from west to east. From AD 81–83 Agricola campaigned north of the Forth of Clyde and defeated the Caledonian tribes under Calgacus at the battle of Mons Graupius in AD 84. Despite this victory there remained a threat to Roman stability from the north. The following year Agricola returned to Rome, where he was to die on 23 August AD 93.

The road heading north reached Ribchester (Bremetennacum) and Hadrian's Wall, following the general route of modern-day Deansgate. Another road headed north-west to Wigan (Coccium). Nearby Castleshaw Roman fort lay 28 kilometres (16 miles) to the east and Northwich (Condate) 29 kilometres (18 miles) to the west. There were also close links to Adrotalia, Slack and Ebchester. There were four main phases of fort construction: the first in c. AD 79–c. AD 90, the second c. AD 90–c. AD 160, the third c. AD 160–c. AD 200, and the fourth c. AD 200–c. AD 400/420. They show the close interaction that seemed to exist between the Roman military fort at Manchester and its neighbouring *vicus*. Mamucium was demolished c. AD 140, with the *vicus* abandoned sometime between c. AD 120–c. AD 160, probably in connection with the demolition of the fort, as the *vicus* was reinhabited when the fort was rebuilt. Towards the end of the first century AD and the beginning of the second the fort was improved, the rampart strengthened, the gateway replaced and the ditch system altered. During this period a tight military grip was maintained upon western Brigantia and the fort became a supply base. The destruction of the fort was possibly as a result of the movement of the garrison north, in order for it to be redeployed in the AD 140s when the Emperor Antoninus Pius occupied southern Scotland.

Higher Campfield Market Hall, from the junction of Liverpool Road and Deansgate, built over an extended *vicus* where key 'finds' have been made.

The second phase of fort development used the same construction methods as the first phase, although it was larger than the previous fort. The increase in size was due to the construction of extra granaries (*horrea*).The third phase of fort development occurred just prior to Emperor Severus's campaign to subdue northern Britain. A larger fort covering 2 hectares (5 acres), with barrack blocks and stone footings, was constructed. It also had stronger ramparts and gates. The fort was probably designed to hold a mixed force of 480 infantry and 128 cavalry. There is evidence of iron-working and locally made pottery, with the economy of the district developing. It is possible the fort was constructed in response to a Brigantian revolt, although this is yet to be proven. Also in this period the frontier along Hadrian's Wall became more stable, which may also account for the fort's expansion. The main feature of the fourth phase of the fort's development is its construction in stone. It would suggest that the fort was completely refurbished, together with many others, under Emperor Severus when he was strengthening the Roman's military presence in the province. The gatehouses were rebuilt in stone and the walls surrounding the fort were faced in the same material. It was similar in size to the previous fort. There is evidence to suggest that Mamucium was still in use in the first half of the third century, although the northern *vicus* was probably abandoned by the mid-to-late third century,

Looking towards the Granaries from Northgate.

based on evidence from reused building materials. Although the *vicus* suffered extensive decline, it is possible a small garrison remained at Mamucium into the late third century and early fourth century. The fort seems to have continued in use until the end of the Roman occupation of Britain.

According to Walker (p. 143) there were increasingly difficult geographical, topographical and environmental challenges facing the Romans by the mid-fourth century, which would have severely impinged upon their ability to effectively operate as coherent military units:

> In the middle of the 4th century the mean sea-level probably reached its greatest height. This should have had the effect of impeding the drainage of the mosses and bogs that surrounded Manchester to the south and west and would consequently have hindered communications. It seems reasonable to suggest, that with the demise of the fort came the demise of the town, so that the very nature of settlement changed radically. The end of the fort marks the end of Roman rule in the area, and the beginning of the Celtic kingdoms.

The reconstructed Northgate of the Roman fort.

Lucius Septimius Severus Pertinax was born on 11 April AD 145–46 at Leptis Magna, Tripolitania (now in Libya) and died on 4 February AD 211 at York (Eboracum). He was Emperor from AD 193–211, creating a personal dynasty and converting the government into a military monarchy. The son of an Equestrian, Severus entered the Senate c. AD 173 and became Consul in AD 190. After the murder of Emperor Commodus in AD 192 and his successor Publius Helvius Pertinax in AD 193, Severus was proclaimed Emperor by his troops and marched on Rome. After the murder of Emperor Julianus, Severus entered Rome unopposed. He replaced the Praetorian Guard with a new 15,000-man guard from his own Danubian legions while his rival in Britain, Albinus, was named Caesar. In AD 194 he marched east, defeating Syria, and then west to defeat Albinus, at Lyon, France, in AD 197. Returning to Rome, Severus executed around thirty of Albinus's senatorial supporters and then late in AD 197 marched east to repulse an invasion of Mesopotamia (Iraq) by the Parthians. By AD 199 the province was annexed to the empire. In AD 208 Severus led an army to Britain in order to extend Roman rule in the north. He died at York in AD 211. Severus gave the army a dominant role in his state and reformed the justice system, his descendants retaining power until AD 235 (with the exception of AD 217–18).

Roeder (pp. 49-56) gives us a 'General View of Mancunium', in which he goes into some detail regarding the appearance and construction of the fort upon its excavation. A contemporary of Roeder's, Dr F. A. Bruton, 'justly recognizes the value of Roeder's work in the book which he edited on the Roman fort at Manchester (1909)'. (Jackson in *Transactions of the Lancashire and Cheshire Antiquarian Society*, vol. XLIX. 1933 pp. 104-12). Roeder's first-hand account is an invaluable primary source relating to the construction and layout of the fort and the urban district that grew up around it. Importantly, the Roman military legacy left by their legions and occupation form a vital part of the historical record today:

The station covered a little over 5 square acres and was of rectangular shape, the corners rounded. It had four detached turrets at its angles, and the walls had an average thickness of 7 feet. It had four gates, irregularly placed, and the northern wall was apparently strengthened by the insertion of six small circular arches at the base. The defences consisted on the northern side of five or perhaps six parallel fosses and small ramparts; on the east side a fosse was drawn round to the Medlock, cut into the rock. The southern side was naturally defended by the curve of the river, whose bank was additionally scarped for greater security, and on the west side rose a lofty bank, skirted by a swampy slope that fell away to the Irwell. The northern wall was built immediately into a swampy hollow, and stood in the first fosse, *without* the appearance of rampart or berme. No trace exists of the gates, which at Melandra were double-arched and had guardrooms attached to them. At the south-east angle were placed the ovens, cut into the rock, and a well was made near the western wall, where probably the altar of the Raetians and Noricians was also placed.The principal buildings, comprising the praetorium, and probably the granary, were about the centre of the station, still indicated by the remnant of a piece of wall, 20 feet long, which has been permanently preserved. The cemeteries followed the margin of the road to Buxton and the stem of the road to Slack and Chester immediately on their issue from the station. Sepulchral monuments on the south side of the Medlock also line the side of the road to Chester. The hypocaust was built on the southern side of the station close to the banks of the river, into which steps were made for access to the water.

The area of the castrum was paved and drained; the south-eastern part, which stood on the rock and was much higher than the north-western part, was levelled with clay and earth. A number of roads issued from the gates – on the eastern side we find the road to Slack (York) and Buxton and to Chester; on the western gate, leading to Woden's Ford or Hulme Bridge, we have the road to Wigan and the estuaries. From the northern gate, near Collier Street, we can yet trace in part the road to Ribchester, which at Hunt's Bank sends off a branch to Blackstone Edge. Outside the station we have on the east side,

The Gatehouse, looking west, showing dedication plinth above the gateways.

The Granaries, looking across the Roman fort to Northgate.

between the wall and the ditch, some important and large buildings that were connected by a paved road with the hypocaust. On the north side of the castrum, rectangular to the Ribchester road, a number of parallel streets were built, reaching up to Camp Street and probably even to Quay Street, the occupied area being defined to the west by Lower Byrom Street. This part of the suburbs was most likely used by the soldiers and traders.

Stepping across Knott Mill we have evidence of a large building and a Roman well at the Crown Inn, (Trafford Street) Gaythorn, has yielded a very rich field of finds – so have Trafford Street and Great Bridgewater Street, which also must have been largely occupied. We must now cross the Medlock; here on its south banks we obtain traces of a water mill and other evidence which makes it clear that it was also populated. We have seen already that the erection at Trafford Street and Gaythorn of *totontini*, and the later construction of a road over the former one, indicates an expansion of the boundaries of the settlement in that direction. Towards Fleet Street and Alport Town, on the east side of Deansgate, the occurrence of finds is remarkably thinning out. Recent excavations have shown that here the original soil is only covered to a slight extent by a layer of Roman "trodden" soil; it seems to have been left in later times to free cultivation, for it is covered with a layer of good light sandy clay almost free from any fragments of pottery.

Taking, now, a general view, the "larger" Mancunium was enclosed and bounded on the west by the Irwell, on the north by Quay Street, on the east by the banks of the Tib, and on the south by the Medlock and certain parts in Hulme alongside the southern banks, perhaps reaching to a little beyond Great Jackson Street.

The station was built by some auxiliary cohorts of the Frisians, we have the names of the first centuria of Masavo, and Quintinianus and Candidus. Those of Candidus and Masavo were seen *in situ* by Camden and Dr. Dee in the walls, while the centurial stone of Quintinianus was found under the rubbish at the eastern gate. Another one of the first centuria of the Frisians (officer's name incomplete) was found at Great Jackson Street, across the Medlock. These three cohorts alone built together seventy-one passus of the compass of the walls, and the general work was probably directed by an officer of the Twentieth Legion, of which a tile was discovered. These troops were all detailed from the headquarters of the chief station at Chester.

Later on we meet with tiles of the Third Cohort of the Bracarae and an altar of the Praep. Vex Raet. et Novic. and another erected by an officer of the Sixth Legion, all of which point to York and the northern Roman wall, and tending to the conclusion that in the following century it was garrisoned not from Chester, but by troops stationed in the north. It is, of course, impossible to define the strength of men by which the station was held. It was never anything but a small third-rate castrum and similar in size (5 acres) to the forts along Hadrian's Wall, which may have held each a complete cohort or ala of nominally one thousand or five hundred men (in some cases certainly one thousand)

The formation of the suburbs probably began in the second century, for most of the earliest ornamental samian pottery scattered over its area, as between Bridge Street and Camp Street, and Gaythorn, Knott Mill, and Hulme, consists of specimens characteristic of types of the second and third century. Of the pottery inside the station nothing can be said, as a systematic search there has never been made. In order to realise the appearance of Castlefield station and its immediate vicinity at that epoch we must keep before us the fact that the whole district in subsequent times has been more or less levelled and artificially covered by 4 feet to 5 feet of soil and rubbish. In its original state the surface was very uneven and its undulating character gave rise to a succession of little hillocks, valleys, and hollows, abounding with pools, springs and rills ...

Later on the more military character of the settlement passed away ... But there was always sufficient stir and bustle to keep the place alive. The traffic and transport of troops from London and Chester to the north must have been unceasing, for the station formed a link in the great artery of the Second and Tenth Iter, and it was a little cosmopolitan beehive, crowded with soldiers, officials, traders, and natives ... the garrison and population enjoyed their full share of opulence and comfort, and, to judge from the enormous amount of pottery and articles found by me alone over a comparatively small area of the suburbs, the accumulation of the articles of daily life must, during a busy occupation, extending over three to four centuries, have become very great. Much has been lost during the last fifty years by indifference and ignorance, but what is left is sufficient to form a slight picture of the interesting life in Mancunium in its best days. (Roeder pp. 49-56)

The Gatehouse, showing its defensive double-ditch system.

The legacy of this military development at Mamucium was one of long-term social and economic change, as a result of the Roman conquest. Walker (pp. 167-181) presented an explanation and description of the role of the first town at Manchester. This article discusses 'acculturation', in which the policy of the empire was to convert new lands into Roman territory and then install new methods of production and trade. He goes on to state that 'during the attempt to convert Brigantia into a Roman province, the fort at Manchester was established. Associated with this fort was a civilian town or *vicus* that was probably founded both to provide facilities for the troops and to act as an administrative centre'. Thus, as a result of the military occupation and establishment of the Roman fort, the foundations of the civilian town that eventually became Manchester were laid.

However, not all Roman settlements survived and prospered post-Roman withdrawal. Mamucium's *vicus* was supported by the neighbouring garrison's wealth and its administrative needs. At Mamucium the *vicus* was abandoned roughly in relation to fort redevelopment, then Roman withdrawal from the north-west, which was not fully 'acculturated.' It would appear that despite Roman abandonment and *vicus* re-establishment and decline at regular intervals in history, the fact that there had been previous and established economic activity close to Mamucium was a spur to future development in more

The Gatehouse and the Northgate fortifications, as seen from the Vicus at Liverpool Road.

recent times. After the Roman withdrawal in the early fifth century and the break-up of the western part of the Roman Empire, there were invasions of Saxons to the south and east and the establishment of new Celtic kingdoms in the north-west. These were the foundations of a new and emerging British society.

Post-Roman Development of Castlefield

For five-hundred years after the Roman garrison's final withdrawal from Manchester the evidence for any occupation of the original settlement is negligible. (Arrowsmith p. 99) It is possible that four features excavated immediately outside the North Gate of the fort were the remains of *grubenhauser*, or Saxon sunken huts, indicating that Manchester was now a rural, and not an urban, community – a sixth-century Saxon cremation urn was discovered at Red Bank, near Victoria Station, and an eighth-century hoard of sceatta (silver Anglo-Saxon coins) was discovered in Tonman Street, near Deansgate, in 1821. According to Arrowsmith, 'each of these might represent no more than casual settlement', therefore making permanent occupation of the *vicus* site in this period unlikely, although Walker (p. 143) suggests that the huts were in use 'before the wall had collapsed and after the fort had been abandoned'. The use of stone from the fort site for other construction purposes dates from the late Saxon period, coinciding with AD 919 when the *Anglo-Saxon Chronicle* tells us that Edward the Elder ordered an army from Mercia to occupy Manchester, then a part of Northumbria. There is some question as to the exact location of this burh – the Roman fort has been suggested as a site. It is possibly 'Aldport,' although Roeder (pp. 126-7) suggests the name originated from the Roman *vicus* and not a Saxon settlement located here, or possibly the rocky spur around Hanging Ditch. Of this period in Manchester's history, Roeder tells us that,

> Mancunium ... disappears from history; some traditionary legends, however, lingered on through many centuries – even reaching into Whitaker's time – of a famous giant Tarquinius, said to have lived in Mancastle, at the Medlock. We have a few Anglo-Saxon sceattas (ranging from 450–600) ... found on the Roman highroad at Campfield, which possibly may fall within the time of the struggle between Eadwin and AEthelfrith, but we are left in darkness until the tenth century, when the Mercians rebuilt Manchester, which had been destroyed by the Danes. No milestones or additional altars, or inscribed stones have been saved from the station, and thus our picture remains blurred. (p. 56)

What is not in any doubt is the fact that Manchester's purpose at this time was a military one, to protect the northern frontier of Mercia from Viking raids.

Whether this occupation led to any permanent settlement of the area is open to question. The Domesday Survey of 1086 mentions only the churches of St Mary, at Manchester,

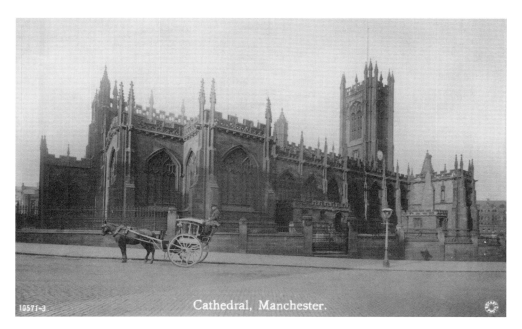

Manchester Cathedral c. 1900. Note the steep incline leading from the River Irwell.

the forerunner of the fifteenth-century Collegiate church, and St Michael, at Ashton-under-Lyne (Arrowsmith p. 100). At some time before 1184 a small castle was constructed at Manchester, probably close to the church and on the site of what is now Chetham's School of Music. By 1282 the castle had gone out of use, to be replaced by a manor house.

Arrowsmith (p. 100) tells us that, 'It is in 1282 that we also have the first evidence of a developing town, in the form of burgage rents amounting to £7 3s 2d. Since each burgage was assessed at a rent of 1s, this total implies the existence of approximately 143 such properties.' On the basis of this calculation and the assumption that one family held each burgage plot, an estimate of a population of around 600 can be made. Salford was granted its charter around 1230 and Manchester 1301, the origins of the two boroughs being 'roughly contemporary'. From these humble origins the town of Manchester grew slowly but steadily. The addition of new burgage plots in the first half of the fourteenth century, through the construction of Long Millgate, which were leased directly from the Lord, aided a growth of Manchester's population. Despite incursions of the Plague in 1348, 1565, 1605 and 1645, which checked population growth, there was steady increase over the next 400 years, with the population of the township of Manchester doubling between the years 1563 and 1664. Manchester established itself as a market town and regional centre, close to the original *vicus*. The presence of a Roman military garrison and then Manchester's later use as a blockade to Viking incursions had at least brought the strategic importance of Manchester to the forefront of people's minds and suggested it as a potential site of settlement. Aided by the strategic importance of the confluence of the

Chetham College in 1904.

rivers Irwell and Medlock as an invaluable transport hub, power source, raw material and domestic supply, and despite the disrepair and ruinous state of the site at Castlefield, the 'old town' near 'Aldport' continued to grow from its thirteenth-century origins. The castle was superseded by burgage plot rents, providing the economic impetus for future growth.

In terms of development of the site into the modern era, after the Romans abandoned their fort and the *vicus* had declined, a new settlement was eventually established around a kilometre to the north-east, on the site of the modern-day Cathedral Conservation Area. The site of the *vicus* became known as 'Aldport', or the 'Old Town'. Much of the area of Roman settlement lay inside Aldport Park, consisting of a large wood, heath, rough pasture, and providing an ecologically biodiverse environment for eagles, hawks, herons and honey-bees. This completely covered the old Roman fort and town. By the eighteenth century the Roman fort was recognizable only as a grass-covered mound. From 1758–61 the Duke of Bridgewater employed James Brindley to construct the Bridgewater Canal, with wharves built c. 1764. The success of the Bridgewater Canal led to the construction of the Rochdale Canal by John Rennie, which cuts through the southern corner of the fort and opened in 1804. Castlefield became the centre of a rapidly developing canal network, which fuelled the growth of Manchester from a market town into an industrial city.

Looking from Castlefield Basin towards Deansgate.

To supply the needs of an increased population a large number of warehouses were built at Castlefield, along the banks of the Rochdale Canal, which intersects one of the corners of the Roman fort and either damaged or destroyed some of the southern half of the fort. By 1750 housing was constructed over large areas of the civilian settlement. Manchester and its population continued to grow and a new means of providing its inhabitants with their needs was found through the construction of railways. The world's first railway station was built on Liverpool Road in 1830 and a network of several railway lines on viaducts was built over the Castlefield area in the nineteenth century. The viaducts were concentrated over the site of the Roman fort, where four viaducts converge, and were extended to Central Station, which opened in 1879/80. When the railway viaducts were built the remains were uncovered in the process, including parts of the *vicus*. Part of Aldport disappeared under the foundations of the Great Northern Warehouse at the end of the nineteenth century. In the twentieth century the station site at Liverpool Road became the Museum of Science and Industry and part of an Urban Heritage Park. At the same time, in 1982, part of the Roman fort was reconstructed on the excavated foundations, including the fort's gatehouse, incorporating some of the original plinth stones, walls, ramparts, granaries and some buildings from the *vicus*, opening in 1984.

Castlefield Basin.

The Gatehouse, looking east.

An extensive archaeological investigation of Mamucium was undertaken by the Manchester Grammar School master Dr Francis Archibald Bruton in 1906, who excavated the fort's western defences. Bruton later worked on the Roman fort and fortlet at Castleshaw – its findings published in 1911 – as well as many other Roman sites across the north-west of England and Wales.

Later, several small-scale excavations were undertaken from 1912–67, concentrating on the northern defences of the fort. The *vicus* was first excavated in the 1970s, when a fragment of a second-century 'word square' was discovered displaying an anagram of PATER NOSTER and possibly of Christian origin. Excavations of the *vicus* again took place in 2001–05, ahead of any regeneration or reconstruction plans. The archaeological examination of the Mamucium Roman fort and its associated *vicus* has so far yielded somewhere in the region of 10,000 artefacts. In March 2008 a very well-preserved altar was found in a pit, possibly a well, near Chester Road on the south side of the River Medlock. The 1-metre-tall altar was probably used as a roadside shrine on the Roman road from Chester (Deva Victrix) and close to the fort at Mamucium. The first Roman stone inscription to be found in Manchester for 150 years, the altar, records only the second known Roman from Manchester – Aelius Victor.

Dr Francis Archibald Bruton (1860–1930) was born in Horsley, Gloucestershire. He moved to Manchester in 1892 to work as an assistant master at Manchester Grammar School, where he taught classics and mathematics. He became a member of the Lancashire and Cheshire Antiquarian Society. The *Manchester Guardian* of 15 January 1930 (p. 14) has his obituary: 'We regret to announce the death, at Weston-Super-Mare, of Dr. Francis Archibald Bruton, Litt D., who for many years was well known in Manchester as a master at the Manchester Grammar School. Dr. Bruton was an authority on Roman Lancashire, had conducted excavations on Roman sites, and had written several works on the Roman occupation of Northern England and kindred subjects. His work at the Grammar School included nature study classes and under his care the school natural history museum grew. From his pen came handbooks to encourage observation in surveying and archaeology, which were used to good purpose in the school camps.' A further Obituary extract from the Manchester Grammar School's magazine, *Ulula*, reads, 'For years past the chapter on Roman Britain in the Classical Association's annual volume, "The Year's Work in Classical Studies," has been written by him. He wrote a survey of Lancashire and a "Short History of Manchester and Salford," and in 1919 a vivid account of the Peterloo "massacre," of 1819.' In retirement he visited Newfoundland, lecturing in Natural History.

The Vicus (right) and the Northgate Gatehouse.

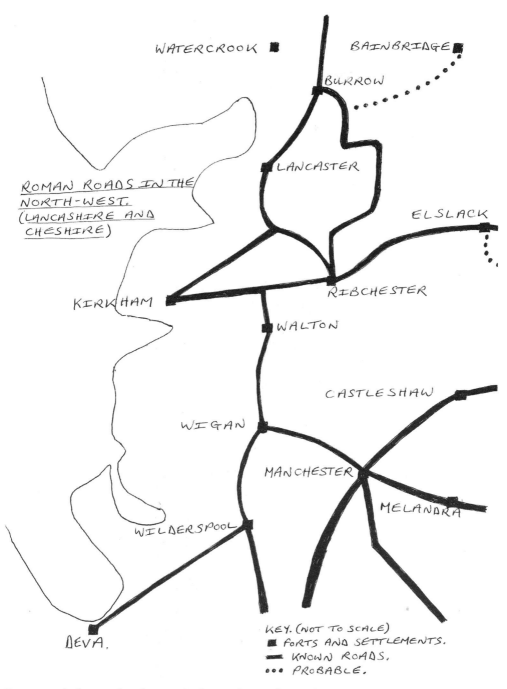

WATERCROOK

BAINBRIDGE

BURROW

LANCASTER

ROMAN ROADS IN THE
NORTH-WEST.
(LANCASHIRE AND
CHESHIRE)

ELSLACK

KIRKHAM

RIBCHESTER

WALTON

CASTLESHAW

WIGAN

MANCHESTER

MELANDRA

WILDERSPOOL

DEVA.

KEY. (NOT TO SCALE)
■ FORTS AND SETTLEMENTS.
▬ KNOWN ROADS.
••• PROBABLE.

Roman roads, forts and settlements in the North West (Lancashire and Cheshire).

Roman Auxiliary infantryman, c. AD 100.

According to the County Archaeologist, Norman Redhead, 'It is the first Roman stone inscription to be found in Manchester for 150 years and records only the second known Roman from Manchester, Aelius Victor – the first being found 400 years ago. The Latin inscription refers to the mother goddesses Henaneftis and Ollototis from Celtic tribes in the Rhineland area of Germany. It is quite possible that Aelius Victor was from this area, recruited into the Roman army and posted to Mamucium. The circular depression on the top of the altar is called the focus and this is where offerings were made to the goddesses in the form of perhaps wine, oil, or even blood. Incense may have been placed here as well.' Today tourism and leisure are the main attractions, making Castlefield, and particularly the reconstructed Roman fort, a popular venue in the twenty-first century.

2. THE SIEGE OF MANCHESTER, 24 SEPTEMBER TO 1 OCTOBER 1642, AND ITS LEGACY FOR THE DEVELOPMENT OF POLITICAL LIBERALISM IN MANCHESTER

The Civil War began on 22 August 1642, when King Charles I raised his standard at Nottingham. The Parliamentarians maintained control of London, East Anglia, most of the Midlands, and all of southern England except West Cornwall. Lancashire was divided. In Manchester the local gentry supported the Parliamentarians, but the local population were mainly Royalist in their sympathies. The most influential local Royalists were Lord Strange (James Stanley, heir to the Earl of Derby), who was the Knowsley-born MP for Liverpool and the main Royalist protagonist in the Siege of Manchester. He had advised

James Stanley, 7th Earl of Derby, and his family, by Sir Anthony Van Dyck (1599–1641).

the King to raise the Royal Standard in Warrington, rather than Nottingham, believing Royalist support had reached its zenith there. However, he was overruled and Manchester and Lancashire were therefore much less involved in the Civil War overall than they might have been. The second most influential Royalist was Sir Alexander Radcliffe of Ordsall Hall, Salford, who was repeatedly fined for refusing to sign the Oath of Protestation opposing the worship of Roman Catholicism. As a result of this opposition he had to sell off much of his property to survive. As the Roman Catholic King Charles I and Protestant-supporting Parliamentarians continually vied for power and control, Manchester, like many other towns, prepared for conflict. Leading landowners recruited men with the initial intention of protecting their own estates, but the long-term aim was of supporting King or Parliament in the impending civil war.

However, not all supported the war, with Richard Heydricke, warden of the Collegiate church of St Mary at Manchester, taking a petition signed by its freeholders to King Charles I, who was then based at York. Whilst this petition had much support and King Charles I was appreciative of their loyalty to the Crown, his response to the signatories was to encourage them to join in the armed struggle against the Parliamentarians. For the freeholders of Manchester, this was not the result they had intended. Manchester's valiant attempt to compromise and avert the Civil War had failed. On 20 June 1642, at a meeting on Preston Moor, those supporting Royalist and Parliamentarians were equally divided, with a similar number of those present undecided. If this was a fair representation of opinions across the whole county, then it would appear that Lancashire was equal in its support of Royalist and Parliamentarian viewpoints. Both sides now went on a frantic search for arms and gunpowder, with the Royalists seizing the magazines at Liverpool, and at Lancaster and Preston, without a struggle. However, Manchester declared for Parliament and refused to hand over its ten barrels to Royalist forces.

James Stanley, Baron Strange, Seventh Earl of Derby (1607–51) was born at Knowsley on 31 January 1607. His family were influential in Lancashire, with his father William Stanley, the 6th Earl of Derby, and his mother Elizabeth de Vere, daughter of the Earl of Oxford. In July 1626 he married Charlotte de la Tremoille. They had six children who survived beyond infancy. In 1642 he became the 7th Earl of Derby and hereditary Lord of the Isle of Man. On 29 September 1651 he was tried by court martial, accused of helping Charles Stuart to invade England. Derby was found guilty and sentenced to death. He appealed for clemency on the grounds that he had surrendered to Captain Edge at Nantwich in 1651, on promise of quarter. But despite the support of Oliver Cromwell, his appeal was rejected. Derby was taken to Bolton where the massacre of 1644, in which he took an active part, occurred. He was beheaded in the market place on 15 October 1651, with his body then buried in the Derby chapel at Ormskirk church.

Lord Strange undertook an urgent Royalist recruitment drive and made it his intention to secure Manchester's gunpowder supplies. These were stored near the Collegiate church of St Mary, and now the site of Chetham's School of Music, close to Victoria Railway Station. However, his attempt came too late, as Sir Ralph Assheton of Middleton had already illegally authorized its removal to other secret locations on 20 June, whilst the meeting at Preston Moor was underway. The ten barrels of gunpowder and three fathoms of match belonged to Lord Strange, as did the Collegiate rooms in which they were stored. These had once been the dwellings of Catholic priests employed in the town. Lord Strange, not surprisingly, was furious at this act and raised a small band of troops, intending to use them to storm into Manchester from neighbouring Bury. He gave the Parliamentarian supporters three days in which to return his gunpowder, or there would be dire consequences. The Parliamentarians refused to accede to Lord Strange's demands and despite rumours to the contrary, Manchester was not attacked on this occasion. However, the town's Parliamentarian defenders were sufficiently disturbed by the close proximity of Lord Strange and his Royalist forces that they raised the number of Manchester militia to 8,000 and drilled them daily.

Victoria Station and Chetham's School of Music (right).

The First Death of the English Civil War, 15 July 1642

On 15 July 1642 Lord Strange arrived for a banquet in Manchester. This was located at the Eagle and Child inn, the home and workplace of Alexander Greene, at The Conduit, now Spring Gardens, close to the junction with Market Street. He arrived in a carriage, flanked by around thirty cavalry riders. Other guests, including Lord Molyneux, brought their own cavalry protection and as the Royalists approached Manchester their forces grew significantly in size. It is true to say that the Royalist presence was not exactly understated as it entered the town. Whilst the banquet was underway the town militia, led by Mr Holcroft, surrounded the inn and a 'stand-off' ensued with the cavalry and footmen. Lord Strange's horse and carriage were confiscated, so that when he left the inn he had to push his way through an angry crowd in order to take Sir Alexander Radcliffe's horse. At this point there were two shots, fired by Thomas Stanley, a kinsman to Lord Strange and a committed Parliamentarian. They came from the upper windows of nearby properties and both missed their target. However, angry clashes now occurred between Parliamentarian-trained militia and Royalist cavalry, although neither side was keen to engage in full-scale hostilities.

Whilst these clashes were taking place Lord Strange rode onto Market Street with the help of his cavalry, who held back the mob. During this exchange one rider was clubbed down from behind and dragged from his horse. The perpetrator was immediately shot dead by one of Lord Strange's men – allegedly Thomas Tyldesley from Astley – and seems to have led to the abatement of the riot. The victim was Richard Perceval, a linen weaver

Market Street from High Street, with Spring Gardens on the left, in 1904.

Sir Alexander Radcliffe (1608–54) sat in the House of Commons from 1628–29. The family seat was at Ordsall Hall in Salford, a predominantly Royalist-supporting town. Ordsall Hall was first recorded in 1177, with the oldest surviving parts of the present hall built in the fifteenth century. The manor first came into the Radcliffe family's possession c. 1335, and they lived at Ordsall Hall for more than 300 years, until it was sold by them in 1662. The Grade I-listed Tudor mansion was originally moated and there were legends of hidden passages from Ordsall Hall, leading to the Manchester bank of the River Irwell, notably at Hanging Bridge. Radcliffe was an ardent supporter of the Royalist cause in the English Civil War. He was later committed to the Tower of London by Parliament for assistance given to Lord Strange in the Siege of Manchester. Radcliffe was the son of Sir John Radcliffe, of Ordsall, Lancashire. He was created Knight of the Bath in 1625, when he was seventeen years old. In 1628 he was elected to Parliament and sat until 1629, when King Charles I decided to govern, without the assistance of Parliament, for the next eleven years.

from 'Kirkmanshulme' and a committed Parliamentarian. He is generally believed to be the first English casualty of the Civil War and was buried in the Manchester Collegiate church on 18 July 1642. Lord Strange continued to ride on to Ordsall Hall, where he spent the night as Sir Alexander Radcliffe's guest. Salford was staunchly pro-Royalist and so he was assured of relative safety at Ordsall. On 16 September 1642 Lord Strange was impeached for the 'murder', with Parliament making the most of this propaganda coup by using the church pulpit to call the civilian population to arms in vengeance. In response, Lord Strange now planned to seize control of the town by raising a Lancastrian force of 3,500 men. However, there was opposition to this plan from King Charles I himself, who was jealous of both Lord Strange's lineage and popularity amongst Royalist supporters. The King requested his presence at court, which was then based at Nottingham. Lord Strange was determined to raise his army first, however.

In Manchester defence preparations were undertaken, led by Robert Bradshaw and William Radcliffe, a relative of Sir Alexander Radcliffe. However, Manchester had no walls or gated entranceways surrounding the town, which made it open to attack. Its Parliamentarian defenders turned to a German mercenary, a military engineer named John (Johan) Rosworm. He had gained his experience of warfare from the current European Thirty Years' War, serving in the Low Countries, and Ireland. He set about building earthwork walls and dug ditches across streets, giving advice to the town's defenders. Chains and bars were also stretched across the streets in order to prevent a cavalry charge through the town and large iron gates were built across the approaches to Market Street. Rosworm also gave advice on the safe storage of potentially volatile gunpowder. Initially he was employed for six months, at a cost of £30. He was eventually

S 2553   THE CATHEDRAL & CROMWELL STATUE. MANCHESTER.

Manchester Cathedral and the Cromwell Monument, c. 1905.

Ordsall Hall, Salford, c. 1900, the seat of the Radcliffe family at the time of the Civil War.

employed for six years, at a cost of £60 a year. Lord Strange attempted to buy Rosworm's services, offering three times whatever Parliament was prepared to pay, but Rosworm bluntly refused. His completed defences were now about to be tested to the full.

The Siege of Manchester, Saturday 24 September to Saturday 1 October 1642

> Saturday, the 24th of September last in the night, came a great company of horse and foot to the number of two or three thousand, against the Towne of Manchester ... with some six or seven canons, came likewise neere unto the Towne. But the Townsmen having some notice on the Saturday Evening of their approach, did send to the Inhabitants thereabouts, who on Sunday and Monday came in abundantly with Muskets, Pikes, Halberts, Staves, and such like, to the number of two thousand.
>
> 'Newes from Manchester, Being a True Relation of the Battell fought before Manchester', in J. Barratt, *The Siege of Manchester 1642*

Lord Strange's forces moved out of Warrington on Saturday 24 September, heading towards Manchester. Bad weather and a broken cannon carriage wheel delayed their advance.

Deansgate from the junction of St John Street, looking towards Manchester Cathedral.

Following the course of the River Mersey until they reached the River Irwell, Lord Strange approached through Salford, with divisions on each side of the river. At Stretford they divided into two units and headed towards Salford Bridge (close to modern-day Victoria Bridge). It was hoped that strong Royalist support in Salford could be used to reinforce their army on the final approach to Manchester town centre. Although the Parliamentarians were well aware of the approaching Royalist forces they allowed them to continue their advance unopposed until they reached Alport Lodge, on Deansgate, near what is now St John Street, at around midnight. These became Lord Strange's headquarters, around a quarter of a mile from Lord Molyneux at Salford Bridge and half a mile from the town (Barratt p. 9) His Pikemen and Musketeers were ill-equipped. Particularly lacking were the Pikemen's corselets (armour), and his request for safe access into the town on the King's business was refused.

Pikemen were equipped with a pike, which was one of the most commonly used weapons on the Civil War battlefield. It consisted of a long wooden shaft, with a steel point on the end. They were inexpensive to produce, soldiers required very little training to use them and they were effective, particularly when used by a co-ordinated infantry unit.

Cathedral Approach (foreground), with Victoria Bridge behind it. Crossing the River Irwell here, Manchester Cathedral is on the left and Salford on the right. The River Irwell and its steep banks proved an effective defence for Manchester's Parliamentarians.

Pikes were supposed to be 16 feet in length, but often soldiers shortened them in order to make their weapon easier to carry. Tactically, Pikemen often formed the front line of an army. As a co-ordinated unit, they would lower their pikes to prevent a cavalry charge from breaking the ranks, thus injuring their horses in the process. Fallen horses would unseat their riders, therefore making them easy targets for musket, or sword. If the army was surrounded then the Pikemen would form a circle, lowering or raising their weapons in an outward-facing defensive 'hedgehog', in order to provide cover. Parliamentarian units defending the unwalled streets of Manchester from Royalist cavalry charges would have undoubtedly drilled in these tactics in the build-up to the siege. As the Civil War progressed the respective Parliamentarian and Royalist cavalry units developed a tactic known as the caracole. This was a manoeuvre whereby the men in the front rank fired their pistols and then rode to the rear to reload. While the front rank were riding to the rear, the second rank rode up to fire and then rode to the rear, while the third rank rode to the front, therefore reducing the effectiveness of the pike as a form of defence.

There were two types of musket available to military units at this time – the matchlock and the flintlock, which could be as long as 5 feet and had a firing range of up to 300 yards. They were both loaded in the same way: gunpowder was poured into the barrel and packed in hard with a stick, and then a lead ball would be put in, followed by wadding to hold the ball in place. To fire the matchlock gunpowder would be emptied into a pan and covered to protect it. A lighted piece of flax would then be pressed into a metal trigger, called the serpent. When the gun was fired the lighted flax in the serpent would come down into the pan and light the gunpowder. The resultant flame would then enter the barrel of the gun and ignite the gunpowder that had been poured into it, thus firing the lead ball. Another matchlock weapon, the caliver, was midway between the size of a musket and a carbine. The wheel-lock, however, whilst being by far the most reliable of these weapons, was also the most expensive. Therefore, this inevitably limited the number used in battle.

Firing the flintlock was slightly easier but more expensive than the matchlock. The pan was filled in the same way, but the serpent contained flint, which produced a spark when it struck the pan, thus igniting the gunpowder. Both weapons were dangerous and clumsy to use, taking time to reload, which, on a battlefield where fortunes were fluctuating rapidly, could be tactically crucial. Some of the longer muskets needed a rest to balance the barrel on because they were too heavy to hold, presenting logistical issues. They were, therefore, to give the Civil War fighting forces some difficult military planning considerations, as they were most effective when a group of musketeers fired a volley of shots at the enemy. Rosworm's unit, defending the Salford Bridge, were about to discover this in the ensuing siege.

At first light on Sunday 25 September, at approximately 4 a.m., the Royalists took up their battle positions. Whilst they were so engaged, Manchester's church bells were rung backwards (Barratt p. 9), as part of a prearranged defence drill calling the men of the town to the front line. The Parliamentarian forces were equally ill-equipped as their Royalist counterparts, using scythes, hoes and rakes where muskets and pikes were

John (Johan) Rosworm was a Dutch, or German, soldier and military engineer, who was known to have been working as a mercenary in Europe from c. 1630–60. Rosworm came to Manchester in 1642. After the town's siege Rosworm organized a counter-attack against the Royalists, capturing Leigh as a base for Parliamentarian forces in Lancashire. As Lieutenant-Colonel in Ralph Assheton's regiment, Rosworm organized the fortification of Preston, following its capture on 9 February 1643. He was retained by Manchester on an annual salary of £60, giving up his commission in Assheton's regiment, and committing himself to improving the garrison's fortifications. Rosworm was involved in the assault on Warrington and fortification of Liverpool, before returning to Manchester. He later fought with Sir Thomas Fairfax at Nantwich and Sir John Meldrum at Liverpool, directing the siege that regained the town on 1 November 1644. By 1648 Rosworm was in financial difficulty and appealed to London for help. However, now that he and his family were living in Manchester, the town would occasionally provide financial assistance. In 1651 he was appointed to a post in New Yarmouth, to oversee preparations for defence against enemy landings. Then on 19 July 1659 he became Engineer General of the Army. There is no further record of him, and it is believed he died in exile following the Restoration.

lacking. However, they held the geographical advantage with the River Irwell's steeply rising bank on the Manchester side making an assault by Royalist cavalry virtually impossible. The same natural river defences had been utilized by the Romans in their siting of the fort of Mamucium at Castlefield. Any advance by Lord Strange would be uphill, with the Parliamentarian defenders making careful strategic use of these risings. Manchester's defenders undoubtedly had some good fortune, as the River Tib – which now flows beneath Tib Street – was in flood, turning much of the immediate vicinity into an impassable waterlogged marsh. This meant that the main areas of Royalist assault were limited to Deansgate, guarded by Lord Assheton and Lord Bradshaw, and Salford Bridge, where a small force commanded by Rosworm had been positioned.

Forces were also positioned at Market Street, led by Captain Richard Radcliffe: 'there was an assault made at the other endes of the towne, especially at the Market Street-Lane end, but were valiantly resisted by Captain Radcliffe and his Company ... our men likewise sallied out, took divers prisoners, slew and put to flight divers that were stragling in the fields.' (*The Siege of Manchester 1642* p. 20).

Whilst Millgate was patrolled by John Booth and Hunt's Bank by Lieutenant Berwick, Shudehill was defended by a division of Parliamentarian soldiers under no specific command. There was little direct engagement on the first day, with Royalist demands and negotiations with Manchester's Parliamentarians achieving little in the way of progress towards direct action or peace. The only significant news came in relation to the

Blackfriars Street bridge, as seen from Victoria Bridge, looking towards Castlefield. Deansgate is beyond the buildings on the left and Salford is on the right. The swollen River Irwell, at this point, proved an effective barrier for Manchester's Parliamentarians, against attacking Royalists.

death of Lord Strange's father, the 6th Earl of Derby, at Chester. This meant that Lord Strange was now the 7th Earl of Derby.

Any Royalist advance would be problematic. Salford Bridge, in particular, afforded little cover other than a small chapel at its halfway point. Parliamentarian musket fire was heavily trained on this feature, although the Royalist's potential cannon fire far outweighed that of the Parliamentarians. Royalist forces had seven small cannon, the Parliamentarians only one, capable of firing balls of 4 and 6lb in weight (Barratt p. 9) However, cannon used in the Civil War tended to be very heavy and difficult to manoeuvre. The largest needed a team of sixteen horses to move it. The Basilisk fired a shot of around 30lb in weight and was thought to have been too heavy for general field service. For this reason they often had to be put into position before a battle began. This would have the effect of alerting any defenders to the fact that the opposition intended to use cannon, thus allowing them to potentially take evasive action, or attempt to capture the ground where the cannons were sited. However, evasive action may have been difficult for those positioned at the exposed Salford Bridge anyway. Missiles fired from these cannons were usually iron balls, but sometimes stones were used. After the cannon had been fired the soldiers operating it had to go through a strict procedure of cleaning and reloading the weapon with ball and gunpowder before it could be fired again. Aiming the weapon was also problematic and so they tended to be employed as a means of instilling fear into the enemy rather than a way of inflicting actual damage.

Much more effective as a weapon of destruction was the mortar, which was easy to manoeuvre and could be operated by one man alone. It fired an explosive shell high into the air, which then detonated on impact. Although it was difficult to train on a given target, the mortar was the most devastating of any weapon used in the Civil War. However, in these very early stages of the campaign they had yet to be deployed in any given numbers. Therefore, on Monday 26 September, after Manchester had rejected Lord Strange's demands for their immediate surrender, the Royalists opened fire with their cannons. Not surprisingly, these proved to be completely ineffective, other than causing some of Rosworm's fifty musketeers to desert. His response was to threaten to personally kill any other man who deserted. In any event there was only one death – that of a spectator who was sitting on a stile too close to the proceedings.

The Royalist advance on Deansgate was checked by their own efforts to hinder the Parliamentarian defence. Smoke from two burning barns and up to ten burning houses now obstructed their view. 'Upon Monday night they burnt a great Barne with much Corne and Hay of M. Grennes, and Some Houses of Master Foxes at the Deanes Gate end.' (*The Siege of Manchester 1642* p. 17) The Royalists had set the barns alight themselves, with the wind initially blowing against the Parliamentarians. However, they had not anticipated that the wind would shift direction, resulting in smoke now being blown against them. The defenders of Manchester were well organized and able to dig in and hold off the assault, aided by this unintended action. This setback and Rosworm's stalwart defence of Salford Bridge were turning the Royalist advance on Manchester into a prolonged siege.

Royalists captured a house on the Salford side of the bridge and now subjected Rosworm's men to intensive all-night musket fire. (Barratt p. 11) Despite rapidly worsening weather conditions, including heavy rain, the Royalists then decided to fire burning faggots onto the rooftops of Manchester's wooden buildings, in the hope that they would set light to them and raze the town to the ground. Not surprisingly, the attempt was unsuccessful but had the effect of alerting Manchester's inhabitants to the fact that their Royalist assailants intended to destroy their town and in all probability would inflict major casualties, in the form of a massacre, in the process. This had the immediate result, therefore, of hardening Parliamentarian defensive resolve. Their fears would appear to be well founded. On 28 May 1644 the Bolton Massacre took place, in which around 1,500 Parliamentarian troops and townspeople were slaughtered by Royalists, commanded by Prince Rupert. Lord Strange was executed in Bolton on 15 October 1651 for his part in this atrocity.

On Tuesday 27 September Salford Bridge again came under attack. Rosworm's musketeers now numbered just fourteen, with desertions continuing; but the Royalists did not seem to be aware of just how critical their opponent's position was. They failed to press

Known as Rupert Count Palatine of the Rhine, Duke of Bavaria, Duke of Cumberland, and Earl of Holderness, he was commonly called Prince Rupert of the Rhine (1619–82). He was a noted German soldier, admiral, scientist (a founder of the Royal Society), sportsman, colonial governor and amateur artist of the seventeenth century. Prince Rupert was the foremost Royalist military commander of the Civil War and an able cavalry commander who saved the Royalists from an early defeat. He was trusted to escort Henrietta Maria to Holland and on his return was given a commission, being made General of the Horse in the Royal Army, aged twenty-three. He remained very loyal to King Charles I throughout the Civil War. However, he was impetuous – a trait particularly prevalent at the Battle of Naseby – but could also be innovative, marching his men at night to break the third Siege of Newark in 1646. Unfortunately, his ego caused division in the Royalist ranks and neglect of those under his command. After the Battle of Naseby in 1645, King Charles I dismissed him from his command but a court martial acquitted him. He then went abroad, returning to England in 1660, King Charles II giving him an annual pension of £6,000, although he continued his military involvement.

home their advantage before enemy reinforcements arrived and Rosworm was able to turn defence into attack. (Barratt p. 11) The house under Royalist occupation at the other end of the bridge was now targeted, Rosworm's men capturing or killing six Royalists, with the loss of two of their own. A lack of communication, disjointed and uncoordinated attacks, and a lack of cohesive leadership had cost the Royalists dear. A blue plaque, erected in 1977 at Victoria Bridge Street, by the Victoria Bridge that crosses the River Irwell between Manchester and Salford, tells us, 'Siege of Manchester (1642). Captains Robert Bradshaw and John Rosworm commanding the town's forces repulsed Royalist troops on the old bridge next to this site.'

Rosworm's personal account of events makes interesting reading and is worth extensive recounting in order to aid our understanding of his contribution to the siege.

My first aime was to set up good Posts and Chains to keep out the Enemies horse; which by the contrivance of a false Alarm, and by the help of the Countreys coming in, upon the ringing of the Bels backwards, devised purposely for this end, I safely performed, though many tongues had doomed me to death, if I ever attempted it. This was done upon Wednesday the 22 of September 1642. Having by this devise drawn some armed men into the Towne, I earnestly pressed, that they might be carefully provided for, heartened and encouraged; for I was confident, that within lesse than a week, that the enemy would make a reall approach, and then these men would stead us; they took my advice; and my prediction fell out accordingly.

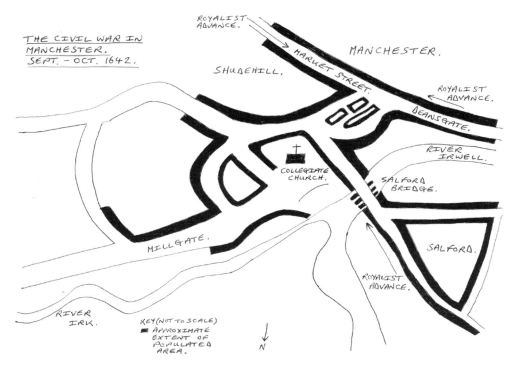

The Civil War in Manchester, September–October 1642. Map showing how Salford Bridge (now Victoria Bridge) was central to the Siege of Manchester.

In that small time of preparation which I had, I fortified and barricaded up every streetes end, with the addition of Mud-Wals, which were unfinished when the Earl came upon us, I advised how our men should be assigned through each part about the Town: But Salford bridge, the onely place of manifest danger, greatest action, and least defence, upon others refusal, I undertook myself: though by my engagements I was not bound to fight at all, but to advise, and direct onely. For this service Septemb. the 26, I took with me 50 Muskettiers: we lay there till Munday without action.

Munday Septb. 27, I was necessitated to send 20 of my Muskettiers to Captain Bradshaw at the Deans-gate which never returned: that afternoon, though thus weakened, I was numerously assaulted: but the goodnesse of him who saved us, my 30 Muskettiers (having no Brest-work but a Chain) gave them a Sound repulse.

The next day, Sept. 28, the Enemy plaid at us with his great Peeces, which being a strange noise, and terrour to my raw men, sixteen of them took to their heels: the rest, some for fear of my drawn sword, others out of gallantry, resolving rather to dye, than to forsake me, stuck close to me, and to the safety of their Town. I was now few in number, but found some pitie from some other gallant hearts, who voluntarily came in to my assistance, making up my number 28. And this was my huge Army even then, when

I had not onely Many Enemies without, but dangerous temptations within to deal with. For the Enemy finding their assault not to take success, nor their Cannons to terrify us, as at the first, severall parleys, some against my will, were sent into the Town: whereof I gave my Souldiers a little notice, with encouragements to stand out to the utmost.

Particularly, Wednesday, September 29, the Earl offered upon the delivery of some 100 muskets to withdraw his Forces, and march away. To back this offer, Colonel Holland, understanding my aversenesse, earnestly pressed me to condescend to the motion, using withall these three reasons. First, he said, we have neither Powder nor Match. I confesse I had onely six pound of the one and 18 fathome of the other: but this was onely known to my self. Secondly, the Countreymen, (Said he, though falsely) will stay no longer, their own horses and goods lying open to the mercy of the Enemy. Thirdly, said he, the Enemy is increased in strength. With these arguments did he not only urge, but almost command the embracing of the Earls proposals. I related these things to my Souldiers, who unanimously resolving never to yield to my Lord of Darby, so long as I would stand out, and they had an inch of Match, or shot of Powder: my heart leaped at such courage, and thereupon I peremptorily refused any terms whatsoever. Which so passionately moved Colonel Holland, that he left me in great anger and discontent. Immediately after this, Master Bourne, an aged and grave Minister came down to the Bridge to me. I told him Colonel Hollands language, and the dangerous concernment it tended to; I advised him, that if he desired to prevent the mischief which might ensue, he would immediately walk to the Deansgate, and from thence to the other centuries, using his best encouragements to prop up their hearts against any dangers, and assuring them from me, that whereas the Enemy now made no assault, but where I was, I was confident with the help of Almighty God, and my few men, to defend it against their whole power, nor should they ever enter at my Guard. The heartened old man quickly left me and followed my advice, with such gravity, and cheerfulnesse, that I cannot but ascribe much to it, as to the meanes of our preservation. Having thus prevailed for a refusal of all terms, sent in by the Enemy, our height of resolution to defend ourselves to the utmost was returned to the Earl: who finding by our actions that we spake as we meant, within 3 dayes after, withdrew this siege, and gave me leave with about ten of my men in open view, to fetch away a great number of good Arms from them. (*The Siege of Manchester 1642*, pp. 22-24)

There were further negotiations on Wednesday 28 September, which had the effect of creating a temporary ceasefire. However, the Royalists continued to attack and plunder any isolated properties on the outskirts of town: 'The Souldier hath ransakt and pillag'd and done abundance of hurt in the country thereabouts.' The Parliamentarians, on the other hand, suffering fatigue due to the prolonged siege, took the opportunity to rest during the ceasefire: 'We have been full of feares, often called out of Bed in the night and in great distresses ...' (*The Siege of Manchester 1642* p. 17) The demands of Lord Strange for the surrender of all arms in Manchester to Royalist control were again declined (Barratt p. 12). However, the Parliamentarians were in a precarious position, running

Victoria Street, Deansgate, looking towards St John Street c. 1900.

low on powder and match, particularly at Deansgate. A unit of 150 foot soldiers was successfully intercepted by the Royalists whilst marching from Bolton in order to reinforce Manchester's Parliamentarian defenders; three were killed. Rumours that Royalist reinforcements were about to arrive, led by King Charles and Prince Rupert, were widespread but untrue. However, demoralization amongst the Parliamentarian ranks was beginning to set in and not everyone was in favour of continuing hostilities.

The Royalists, however, were not without their setbacks. On Thursday 29 September a Royalist officer, Captain Standish, was instantly killed by a musket ball fired by a Parliamentarian musketeer on the steeple of what is now Manchester Cathedral. The victim was on the Salford side of the River Irwell, and was shot at a considerable range. The loss of this popular officer had a significant negative effect on the resolve of the Royalist units under his command, so much so that they began to desert en masse. (Barratt p. 13) One final push along Deansgate was made by counter-attacking Royalist forces, whose failure to capture the town now meant that they were low on ammunition and food supplies. The Parliamentarians' initial assault saw an intensive attack on Salford Bridge, recapturing a house that had fallen under Royalist control. During the successful rout three men, including a Captain Snell, drowned in the River Irwell whilst trying to escape. The river was fast-flowing and swollen by floodwater at the time. Although Royalist forces continued to fight throughout Friday 30 September, this proved to be the last significant act of the campaign. Firing remained half-hearted at

Born in Fife on 19 November 1600, Charles I was King of England, Scotland and Ireland from 27 March 1625 until his execution on 30 January 1649. Charles was the second son of King James VI of Scotland and Anne of Denmark, but after his father inherited the English throne in 1603, he moved to England. He became heir apparent to the English, Irish and Scottish thrones on the death of his elder brother, Henry Frederick, Prince of Wales, in 1612. An unsuccessful and unpopular attempt to marry him to the Spanish Habsburg princess, Maria Anna, culminated in an eight-month visit to Spain in 1623, which merely confirmed there would be no prospects of success in these marriage negotiations. Two years later he married the Bourbon princess, Henrietta Maria of France, three months after his accession, the intention being to establish a treaty and alliance with France at the expense of Spain. They left five surviving children. There was tension over Charles I's unpopular friendship with George Villiers, the Duke of Buckingham (assassinated 1628), and with Parliament over money and religious differences. In 1629 Charles dissolved Parliament, which was not recalled for eleven years, when there was unrest in Scotland and Ireland. He unsuccessfully attempted to arrest five members of Parliament and in August 1642 civil war began. Arrested by the Scots in 1646 and returned to England, he escaped to the Isle of Wight in 1647, with the Second Civil War also unsuccessful. Arrested and tried, he was executed outside the Banqueting House on Whitehall, London.

Manchester Cathedral and steeple, as seen from the River Irwell, and giving us an indication of its height and unrestricted views of the immediate vicinity of Deansgate in the seventeenth century.

best and defensive trenches on Deansgate were now dug in order to screen the Royalists whilst they made a tactical retreat.

An exchange of prisoners took place on Saturday 1 October, as the Royalists now accepted that they had been unsuccessful in their attempt to capture Manchester. The town's defenders released their Royalist prisoners, whilst Lord Strange responded with the release of Parliamentarian captives, before retreating rapidly. However, he left behind valuable gunpowder, weapons and miscellaneous supplies, which now fell into Parliamentarian hands. Royalist losses were estimated to be in the region of 150, whilst the Parliamentarians lost approximately twenty of their men. The wet weather conditions had conspired against the Royalists, preventing them from razing Manchester to the ground, or deploying their cavalry across a wider expanse of the unwalled town in order to attack from several directions or encircle the Parliamentarians in a pincer movement. Waterlogged ground hampered their progress, as did swollen rivers caused by floodwater, which made fording impossible. It is also probable that water affected the gunpowder supplies of the Royalists and flooded their powder stores. Royalist morale was affected by prolonged exposure to the wet conditions, without adequate shelter. No blockade of the town had been attempted and assaults were concentrated on the strongest points of defence, not the weakest. 'Regular' Royalist infantry was also urgently required by the king's main field army, thus making an extended siege unlikely.

On 10 October 1642 Parliament issued an official vote of thanks to the defenders of Manchester, which stated that,

> Tis not unknown to all the Kingdom that Manchester men, since the beginning of these distractions, have behaved themselves like men, and to their lasting fame, have expressed themselves faithful servants to the Parliament in defending their privileges. (Dore p. 16)

Despite this early conflict there were no more direct attacks on Manchester, which remained heavily defended for the duration of the Civil War. However, Manchester did not escape wartime damage completely. Upon sequestration of the Collegiate church in 1649, it was severely ransacked by Roundheads. They smashed stained-glass windows and a statue of Bishop Oldham. Heydricke, still warden of the church, was arrested and removed to London, where he was charged with plotting to reintroduce the monarchy. He was stripped of his position and was lucky to escape the death sentence. On his reinstatement he introduced the *Classis* to Lancashire, dividing the county into nine ecclesiastical districts, although the system was discontinued in 1653. The legacy of this conflict was to have far-reaching consequences for Manchester, well into the nineteenth century. On Charles II's restoration, the right of Manchester to send any MPs to Parliament was removed, as a punishment for their support of the Parliamentarians in the Civil War and the Siege of 1642. They were not to regain any political representation until the Reform Act of 1832.

Oliver Cromwell was born in Huntingdon on 25 April 1599 and died at Whitehall, on 3 September 1658. In August 1620 he married Elizabeth Bourchier at St Giles Church, in Cripplegate, London. They produced nine children. Elizabeth was born in 1598 and died in November 1665. Cromwell was elected to Parliament in 1628 and 1640. He was a Puritan who helped to organize Parliamentarian armed forces after the outbreak of civil war in 1642. He served as a Deputy Commander of the New Model Army, which conclusively defeated the main Royalist force at the 1645 Battle of Naseby. After the death of King Charles I, Cromwell served in the Rump Parliament and set about reforming the legal system. This was partly achieved by the establishment of the Blue Laws of 1650 against blasphemy, cursing, drunkenness and adultery. He commanded campaigns in Ireland and Scotland in the early 1650s and served as Lord Protector of England, Wales, Scotland and Ireland from 1653 until his death in 1658. His power was based around his military ability and close relationship with his troops; he always led his Ironsides from the front. In 1645 he backed the formation of a standing army, with central funding and control. The resultant New Model Army, under the command of Thomas Fairfax (and Cromwell as his deputy), crushed the Royalists at Naseby and forced King Charles I to surrender within a year. In religious matters he believed in liberty of conscience for his fellow Christians.

The Cromwell Monument and Exchange Station in 1909.

In 1874 a bust of Oliver Cromwell, sculpted by Matthew Noble, was presented to Manchester City Council by Thomas Bayley Potter MP and placed in the town hall. The following year a statue of Cromwell, also by Matthew Noble, was placed close to Manchester Cathedral. This was to prove a controversial move. Queen Victoria refused to visit the city to open the new Manchester town hall unless the statue was removed. Manchester's large immigrant Irish Catholic population, reminded of Cromwellian massacres during Ireland's rebellion, were offended by the statue and considered it an affront to their nationality and religion. However, the statue was to remain in situ until it was moved to Wythenshawe Park in 1968.

The Siege of Wythenshawe Hall, 21 November 1643 to 25 February 1644

Prince Rupert and the 7th Earl of Derby set up camp on the Lancashire and Cheshire border, at a strategically safe distance from Manchester. Support came from nearby Wythenshawe Hall, owned by Robert Tatton. He had recruited many of the Royalist troops that marched on Manchester to besiege the town, and realized that he would

Wythenshawe Hall in 1978.

be an easy target for any Parliamentarian reprisals. Once the siege was over and the Royalists were in retreat, he began to build defences against possible attack, clearing out the original moat that surrounded the hall. Many local friends, supporters and servants came to assist in this task and were to help in the defence of the property when the Parliamentarians made several attempts to overcome the Royalist defenders. The siege was to last for three months, with the Parliamentarians failing to overcome some fairly rudimentary defences, including bows and arrows. Whilst Thomas Gerrard of Timperley was bringing food to the house he shot himself in the thigh, such was the inexperience of many of those involved. Another occupant was heavily pregnant throughout the siege.

The extreme winter weather favoured Wythenshawe Hall's defenders, whilst the Parliamentarians were very inexperienced. Their best troops were away fighting at the Battle of Nantwich, leaving around 100 men pitched against a well-fortified and moated hall stocked with enough arms and food to sit out a long siege. At the height of the siege there were approximately fifty-two people stationed at Wythenshawe Hall, including twenty-five domestic household servants and sixteen freeholders. At one stage the Royalists asked for a truce so that they could recover their dead and give them a Christian burial, but were refused by the Roundheads. They were buried in unconsecrated ground close to the hall and at much risk to the gravediggers.

Oliver Cromwell rose rapidly through the military ranks. The Parliamentarian armies achieved stunning victories under his command. His joint leadership (as deputy) of the New Model Army with Sir Thomas Fairfax also allowed him to learn from the experience of an established commander. Cromwell and his Ironsides (later the cavalry of the Eastern Association) developed their own unique approach to warfare, one which was to progress further with the New Model Army and victory at Marston Moor. The forces of Cromwell were disciplined and truly formidable opponents. 'His men were Harquebusiers [i.e. armed with a harquebus, or carbine], the only heavy cavalry on the Civil War battlefield. Clad in a buff coat, a back and breast plate and a triple-barred lobster-tail helmet, they were armed with a heavy, straight-bladed sword and a short musket or carbine and two pistols.' (Bennett p. 25) Both sides would have cavalrymen that came within Bennett's description. However, what differed was the way they were led. Cromwell and Fairfax marshalled their forces from the front, and were able to take a disciplined unit over great geographical distances, in order to keep the pressure on their Royalist counterparts. This enabled them to deliver a 'second blow' to the enemy with their reserve force, even after hard-won victories. Indeed, it was the arrival of further forces at Wythenshawe Hall that eventually broke the siege.

Thomas, Lord Fairfax.

Roundheads attacking in a Civil War re-enactment. (Photo Barry Skeates)

However, those besieging Wythenshawe Hall did not benefit from the progressive leadership developed amongst the Roundhead ranks. Despite sporadic skirmishing, including one incident when Roundheads battled their way into the kitchen of the hall and killed six defenders before being beaten back, it was the arrival of Thomas Fairfax that eventually broke the Royalist resolve. His division arrived at the hall on 25 February 1644. Two cannons were trained on the hall and the threat was issued that the Parliamentarians would raze the property to the ground if surrender was not forthcoming. The Royalists had no protection against such firepower and surrendered immediately, as they had exhausted their supplies of food, water and ammunition. However, Sir Robert Tatton had by this time escaped, and later joined the king in the unsuccessful battle for Chester. Wythenshawe Hall was returned to the Tatton family two years later after they had paid a substantial fine.

During the siege the fiancé of a servant named Mary Webb was killed. Legend tells us that in revenge she took a musket and shot dead a Colonel Adams who was sitting on a wall. There is a ghost connected to this incident, which is said to roam the hall to this day. Wythenshawe Hall was home to the Tatton family for over six hundred years. Together with 250 acres of parkland, it was given to the city of Manchester by Lord and Lady Simon in 1926. The former Royalist civil war stronghold thus became part of the legacy of former Parliamentarian Manchester. A devastating fire in March 2016 severely damaged the hall, but repair and renovation work are currently being undertaken so that the public may continue to enjoy this historic landmark.

Sir Thomas Fairfax, 3rd Lord Fairfax (1612–71) was a leading Parliamentarian of the First and Second Civil Wars and Lord-General of the New Model Army. He refused to fight against Charles II in the Third Civil War and supported the Restoration. He was born at Denton Hall, near Otley, Yorkshire, on 17 January 1612 and married Anne, the daughter of Sir Horace Vere, in June 1637. They had two daughters. In January 1645 Fairfax became Commander-in-Chief of the newly formed New Model Army. Under his leadership it quickly became an efficient and disciplined fighting force. On 14 June 1645 the deciding battle of the English Civil War was fought at Naseby. Fairfax's involvement was crucial, heading several cavalry charges and personally capturing the colours of Prince Rupert's Bluecoat Regiment. He then marched into the Royalist-held West Country, defeating Goring at Langport in July and taking Bristol in September 1645. Fairfax captured Dartmouth in January 1646 and defeated the Royalists at Torrington. Then on 13 March 1646 he accepted Hopton's surrender at Truro. Finally, on 24 June 1646, the Royalist's headquarters at Oxford surrendered to Fairfax, ending the First Civil War.

3. THE PETERLOO MASSACRE, 16 AUGUST 1819, AND ITS LEGACY FOR THE ESTABLISHMENT OF NATIONAL POLITICAL FREEDOMS

Structure of the Manchester and Salford Yeomanry and Build-up to the Massacre

Henry Hunt – To the inhabitants of Manchester and neighbourhood. Our enemies are exulting at the victory they profess to have obtained over us, in consequence of the post-ponement for a week, of the public meeting intended to have been held on Monday last ... our enemies will seek every opportunity by the means of their sanguinary agents to excite a riot, that they may have a pretence for spilling our blood, reckless of the awful and certain retaliation that would certainly fall on their heads ... come then, my friends, to the meeting on Monday, armed with no other weapon but that of a self-approving conscience; determined not to suffer yourselves to be irritated or excited by any means whatsoever to commit any breach of the public peace.

Bill produced by the *Manchester Observer,* Wednesday August 11 1819

The Peterloo Massacre was ironically named after the Duke of Wellington's famous victory at Waterloo, which had been fought only four years before on 18 June 1815, the inference being that the Manchester and Salford Yeomanry, whose alleged incompetence was responsible for the massacre, had 'bravely' charged into a large gathering of unarmed protesters and put many, including women and children, to the sword.

But who were the Manchester and Salford Yeomanry? The use of cavalry and infantry to put down civil disturbances, protect property and disperse rioting crowds was general practice long before the incident at St Peter's Fields. Peterloo did not deter their employ-ment in subsequent disturbances either, including the Chartist demonstrations some twenty years later. In fact, Manchester was regarded as such a 'hotspot' for potential riot-ing that 2,000 troops were permanently stationed there. Notorious disturbances which added to this reputation included riots at Shude Hill in 1757 and 1812, and disorder at neighbouring Stockport, also in 1812, as a result of the great depression. On 10 March 1817 an assembly of people in St Peter's Fields intended to undertake the Blanketeers march of petitioners to London. The Cheshire Yeomanry were called out as a result. They were an important element in quelling civil disturbances in an urban and industrial district, with the farmers and country squires making up its ranks especially keen to preserve the Corn Laws, which the Reformers wanted repealing. The King's Dragoon Guards surrounded

Cavalry charge at Waterloo.

the speakers and constables took them all into custody. No opposition was offered to the cavalry, the crowd quickly dispersed and, unlike Peterloo, the troops gave them free passage. However, the marchers were harassed all the way to Macclesfield, where more were arrested. In September 1818 the Dragoons were again called out to disperse locked-out spinners who were attacking a mill in Ancoats. In 1819 'machine riots' occurred at Middleton, whose population also took a very active part in the events of Peterloo in the same year.

The Manchester and Salford Yeomanry were founded in 1817, with 116 involved on the day of the massacre. They were nearly all from Manchester, with a small number from Pendleton and Stretford. Their occupations included tradesmen, innkeepers and small manufacturers such as cheesemongers, ironmongers, tailors, watchmakers, calico printers, butchers, corn merchants and butter factors. It is unlikely, on this evidence, that many were skilled horsemen, an important factor in the events of Peterloo. They lacked the knowledge and experience of regular calvary and took their orders from civil authorities, whose hasty judgement escalated the situation to critical levels. It would be useful to look at the background of a typical volunteer, in order to more fully understand their motivation for joining what were essentially establishment-sponsored paramilitary units. William Hallsworth of Ancoats was my five-times great-grandfather, and whilst he was not a cavalryman of the Manchester and Salford Yeomanry, his membership of the Second Battalion of the Manchester and Salford Volunteers is worthy of note.

William was the landlord of the Sir Ralph Abercrombie public house on Great Ancoats Street. He had made his fortune as a silk handloom weaver in the boom years before the Napoleonic Wars, but invested his money in business. His main investment was in his public house, which remained in the family until c. 1865. He also traded as Dewhurst & Hallsworth, fustian calenderers, of Hallsworth Court, owned and rented out the majority of properties on Hallsworth Street (now Old Mill Street), owned further properties in Liverpool and traded out of retail properties in Manchester. As a resident of Ancoats, he would have borne witness to the increasing civil unrest in the area between workers and mill owners using lockouts against factory spinners. As a Manchester and Salford Volunteer, it is possible that he was involved in similar activities to the Yeomanry in 1819. Volunteer forces were operational between the years 1794–1813 and were completely disbanded by 1816. William's first record of involvement with the Second Battalion of the Manchester and Salford Volunteers is in the *London Gazette* of 24 October 1801, where he is noted as a gentleman 'to be Quarter-Master'. This was a regimental officer, usually a captain or major, commissioned from the ranks traditionally, and responsible for looking after supplies. It is likely, therefore, that William had been a part of the Second Battalion since the inception of the unit, around 1794. By 1816 at the latest, the battalion had been disbanded, with the Manchester and Salford Yeomanry established in 1817.

The next record belonging to William Hallsworth is noted in the *Lancaster Gazette* of 13 August 1825 (p. 3) telling us of his death: 'On the 29th ult. Mr. William Hallsworth, in the 68th year of his age, late Adjutant in the second battalion of Manchester and Salford Volunteers.' An adjutant is a military officer who acts as an administrative assistant and aide to a senior officer, and is responsible especially for correspondence and written orders. Usually a senior captain, or sometimes a major, as the colonel's personal staff officer an adjutant was in charge of all the organization, administration and discipline for a battalion or regiment. Therefore, by the time of the battalion's disbanding around 1816, William had been promoted to a senior rank. The most significant factor relating to William's career in the Manchester and Salford Volunteers is that his death notice emphasizes his role as an adjutant in the Second Battalion. Bearing in mind his extensive roles in the community as a landlord, property owner and businessman, his specific noting of a military background shows us just how important this role was to the entrepreneurial Mancunian, both in terms of prestige and protection of their assets. Whilst I am by no means excusing the actions of the Manchester and Salford Yeomanry at Peterloo, when we look at the mindset of William and his contemporaries it is not difficult to understand how their conservative anti-reformist political beliefs, pride and over-enthusiasm, coupled with their lack of field experience and desire to settle old scores, could lead to disaster.

The extreme social divisions between the Reformers and Yeomanry were emphasized by the Yeomanry's comparative privilege and the Reformers' relative poverty at the time of Peterloo. Bruton (p. 86) quotes a passage from an article in the *Manchester Observer*, which was published one month before Peterloo, and gives us an indication as to the contempt felt by certain sectors of Manchester's public for the Volunteers:

> The stupid boobies of Yeomanry cavalry in the neighbourhood have only just made the discovery that the mind and muscle of the country are at length united, and during the past week have been foaming and broiling themselves to death in getting their swords ground and their pistols examined ... The Yeomanry are, generally speaking, the fawning dependents of the great, with a few fools and a greater proportion of coxcombs, who imagine they acquire considerable importance by wearing regimentals.

The radical rhetoric of the reformist press; the Yeomanry's use of the same cutler to sharpen their weapons, suggesting a pre-meditated act, with the intention of violence; the Cheshire Yeomanry's orders to be ready at a moment's notice to aid the civil power; and the Reformers' use of drilling before the meeting in order to produce a calm, disciplined and methodical approach to it, seen as illegal by the authorities, all added to the tension before 16 August.

Peterloo occurred on Monday 16 August 1819 on a large area of open land close to the modern-day St Peter's Square in city centre Manchester. The area is now occupied by the frontage of the old Central Station – now an exhibition centre – the old Midland Hotel, and Peter Street, crossing it as far as the Friends' Meeting House and Central Library.

St Peter's Church, St Peter's Square, Mosley Street, in 1890. Peter Street and the site of St Peter's Fields are on the left of this image.

Front of the old Central Station, the site of the speakers' hustings in 1819.

The old Midland Hotel, looking towards Windmill Street from St Peter's Square. This building covers part of St Peter's Fields, where the protesters gathered in 1819.

Peter Street, part of which formed St Peter's Fields, where the protesters gathered in 1819.

The Friends' Meeting House, Mount Street.

A red plaque on the front of the Free Trade Hall, Peter Street, commemorates the massacre. It reads, 'ST. PETER'S FIELDS. THE PETERLOO MASSACRE. On 16th August 1819 a peaceful rally of 60,000 pro-democracy reformers, men, women and children, was attacked by armed cavalry resulting in 15 deaths and over 600 injuries.' Around fifteen people, including a woman and a child, died from wounds inflicted by sabres. These are heavy cavalry swords, with a slightly curved blade that is sharp along one edge. Trampling, caused presumably by cavalry horses and the panic initiated by the cavalry charge, was also responsible for many of the more serious injuries. The massacre occurred during 'a period of immense political tension and mass protests. Fewer than two percent of the population had the vote, and hunger was rife with the disastrous Corn Laws making bread unaffordable'. Bruton (p. 81) tells us that, 'at the conclusion of the Napoleonic War the Corn Bill led to fresh disturbances, which continued, more or less, up to the date of Peterloo, the chief causes being unemployment, the scarcity of food, and the terrible social and economic conditions under which the operatives and their families lived'.

Commemorative plaque on the Free Trade Hall, Peter Street.

The chapel dedicated to the Manchester Regiment in the Manchester Cathedral. (Photo Mister Oy)

Above: Charles I and Queen Henrietta Maria by Sir Anthony Van Dyck.

Left: An ultra-realistic re-enactment: the Earl of Manchester's regiment of foote in a Civil War action. (Photo Paul Stevenson)

Prince Rupert of the Rhine.

Oliver Cromwell and the executed Charles I, by Paul Delaroche (1797–1856).

Typical Hussar cavalryman of the early nineteenth century.

C Company, 2nd Battalion, the Manchester Regiment taking a German battery at Francilly Sellency, April 1917, by Richard Caton Woodville.

Lancaster Bomber the *Phantom of the Ruhr* produced at Trafford Park.

The Royal Regiment of Fusiliers exercising their Freedom of the City in Rochdale, Greater Manchester, 2009. (Photos Adam Kerfoot-Roberts)

Sergeant-Major George Evans VC (1876–1937) of the Manchester Regiment was a recipient of the Victoria Cross for his action of 30 July 1916 during the Battle of the Somme. This is his grave at Beckenham Cemetery, Bromley, UK. (Photo Rocky Biggs). *Inset*: The Victoria Cross.

The Free Trade Hall, Peter Street, now a hotel.

The Corn Laws were a series of statutes, in force from 1815–46, which kept corn prices at high levels. Their purpose was to protect English farmers from cheap foreign imports of grain after the Napoleonic Wars. During these wars Britain blockaded Europe, intending to isolate Napoleon's empire and bring economic hardship to the French. Goods in Britain were therefore protected from outside competition. Farming became very lucrative and land prices increased. In 1815 the war ended and the Corn Laws were introduced. No foreign corn was allowed into Britain until domestic corn reached a price of 80 shillings per quarter. The nobility and other large landowners benefited and had a vested interest in their continuing. The right to vote depended on land ownership, meaning voting members of Parliament did not want the Corn Laws repealed. The urban working class suffered from high corn prices, their wages leaving nothing left for the purchase of manufactured goods, which meant manufacturers had to lay off workers. Unemployment exacerbated the downward economic spiral. The first attempt at reform in 1828 failed. The 1832 Reform Act extended the right to vote to a large sector of the merchant class, who demanded change to the Corn Laws. The Chartists and the Anti-Corn Law League also demanded change and other social reforms. In 1846, the government, under Sir Robert Peel, rescinded the Corn Laws.

Over the weekend leading up to the meeting on the Monday, there was a steady stream of people arriving in Manchester. No disturbance of any kind took place in this period but the authorities appeared to be in a panic over the sudden influx. A notice recommended that local inhabitants were to remain in their houses all day and keep their children and servants indoors. Shop windows and the lower windows of dwellings were shuttered and boarded as a precaution. There was a general feeling of apprehension in the town whilst preparations were made for the meeting. Reformers began to gather in the morning from around nine o'clock, descending on St Peter's Fields from all over the Manchester area and beyond. Many were wearing their Sunday best and all were peaceful, with bands playing and women and children dancing. The main speaker was Henry Hunt, whose speaking platform was a cart, in front of what is now the G-Mex Centre (Manchester Central Convention Complex). Banners were to be placed at these hustings, brought to the meeting by the Reformers themselves, and asking for 'Reform, Universal Suffrage, Equal Representation and Love'. Significant to the course of events was the use of the red cap of liberty that topped many of the banner poles. Their presence was a powerful democratic symbol at the time.

Local magistrates met first at the Star Inn, moving at eleven o'clock to Mr Buxton's house in Mount Street, where they watched the demonstration develop from a window overlooking St Peter's Fields. They were to later panic at the sight of a near 60,000 crowd and allegedly read the Riot Act, which meant that those who were close enough to hear it, if indeed it was read, would have a maximum of one hour to disperse.

Central Station, Windmill Street, in 1902.

Henry 'Orator' Hunt was a radical speaker who pioneered working-class radicalism and influenced the later Chartist movement. Hunt supported Parliamentary reform and the repeal of the Corn Laws. Born in Upavon on 6 November 1773, on his father's death in 1797 he inherited the family estates in Wiltshire and Somerset. Hunt was involved in a dispute which led to him being imprisoned for six weeks. During his court case Hunt was introduced to radical lawyer Henry Clifford, a supporter of the campaign for adult suffrage, who in turn introduced Hunt to his political associates. Hunt became involved in radical politics, gaining a reputation as a passionate public speaker. After Peterloo, Hunt was arrested and found guilty of unlawful assembly and inciting a riot and sentenced to two and a half years imprisonment at Ilchester Gaol. After his release in October 1822, Hunt continued agitating for adult suffrage. He formed the Radical Reform Association with William Cobbett, and stood for Parliament as a radical. In 1830 he stood as the radical candidate for Preston, which had given the vote to all tax-paying males. His winning campaign included a ten-hour working day and an end to child labour. After his victory, 16,000 marched to Manchester and held a meeting at the site of the Peterloo Massacre. In 1832, he opposed the Reform Act, as it did not grant the vote to working-class men, which upset some radicals, and led to his defeat in the general election of the following year. Hunt retired to Whitchurch, Hampshire, where he died on 15 February 1835.

Mount Street from the Friends' Meeting House, looking towards St Peter's Fields and the site of the protest in 1819.

The Massacre at St Peter's Fields

Waiting in reserve were 600 Hussars, several hundred infantrymen, an artillery unit with two six-pounder guns, 400 men of the Cheshire cavalry and 400 special constables. The local Manchester and Salford Yeomanry, led by Captain Hugh Birley and Major Thomas Trafford, were charged with the task of arresting the speakers. Essentially they were a paramilitary force, drawn from the ranks of the local mill and shop owners, who were not used to controlling large crowds of people whilst manoeuvring them on horseback. As local people, they were familiar, and had old scores to settle with many of the protesters – the press in particular. This fact in itself led to problems regarding discipline on the day. The *London Times* tells us of an incident that occurred during the Yeomanry advance upon the hustings:

> A person of the name of Saxton, who is, we believe, the editor of the *Manchester Observer*, was standing in the cart. Two privates rode up to him. 'There,' said one of them, 'is that villain, Saxton: do you run him through the body.' 'No,' replied the other, 'I had rather not – I leave it to you.' The man immediately made a lunge at Saxton, and it was only by slipping aside that the blow missed his life. As it was, it cut his coat and waistcoat, but fortunately did him no other injury.

Hugh Hornby Birley was born in Blackburn on 10 March 1778. He owned a large textile factory on Oxford Road. Birley had a reputation for extremist political opinions and was a captain in the Manchester and Salford Yeomanry, which he had previously used to disperse weavers marching from Manchester to Ashton-under-Lyne. During an industrial dispute at his factory in 1818, Birley was involved in a violent altercation with some of his workers, who attacked his factory with stones. Therefore, by the time of Peterloo, Birley had an already established hatred of reformers. He was Major Thomas Trafford's second-in-command at Peterloo, and carried out the order to arrest the speakers at St Peter's Fields. Some eyewitnesses stated that most of the sixty men whom Birley led into the crowd were drunk. Birley later claimed that the cavalry's undisciplined arrival at the meeting was due to the Yeomanry horses being afraid of the noisy crowd. Journalists, particularly John Tyas of the *London Times*, accused Birley of using unnecessary force whilst arresting the speakers and of being directly responsible for the deaths of demonstrators. It was also claimed that there was a deliberate co-ordinated effort to kill several well-known radicals in the crowd, as well as journalists, particularly the editor of the *Manchester Observer*. In April 1822 a court case was brought against Birley and three others by Thomas Redford, who had been badly wounded. Despite damaging evidence, they were acquitted. Birley continued to live in the town and became Manchester's first president of the Chamber of Commerce. He died on 31 July 1845.

By the time the magistrates had taken up their positions at Buxton's house, the troops had been posted out of sight in the streets around St Peter's Fields. One troop of Yeomanry was positioned in Pickford's Yard, off Portland Street, commanded by Captain Birley; another was posted in Byrom Street, commanded by Major Trafford. The Cheshire Yeomanry were at full strength, with eight troops (400 men) stationed at St John Street. Two squadrons of the 15th Hussars (over 300 men) were in Byrom Street. A further troop was in Lower Mosley Street escorting a troop of the Royal Horse Artillery with two long six-pounders. The 31st Infantry were in Brazennose Street and several companies of the 88th Infantry were stationed along Dickinson Street. The whole force was under the direction of Lieutenant-Colonel L'Estrange. At twelve o'clock a double cordon of around 400 special constables was formed between Buxton's house in Mount Street and the hustings, which allowed the magistrates to communicate with the speakers if required. The magistrates drew up a statement that the town was in danger and instructed the Deputy Constable, Nadin, to arrest the leaders. Nadin responded by stating that he could not do this without military assistance and so the magistrates retained the Manchester and Salford Yeomanry under their own control, in order to support a civil arrest.

For two hours the Yeomanry and Hussars remained at their stations dismounted. Occasionally several of the officers would ride up to Deansgate to watch the procession. Protesters were packed closely together and marching at an even pace, with their banners unfurled and bands playing. Henry Hunt was in an open carriage adorned with flags and

Chartism arose out of the failure of the 1832 Reform Act to offer the vote to all and not just to property owners. In 1838 a people's charter was drawn up for the London Working Men's Association by William Lovett and Francis Place, demanding male suffrage, secret ballots, Parliamentary elections every year, constituencies of equal size, paid MPs and the abolition of the property qualification for MPs. In June 1839 the petition was presented to the House of Commons and rejected. Violence followed, swiftly put down by the authorities. A second petition was presented in May 1842. This was again rejected, resulting in more unrest and arrests. In April 1848 a third and final petition was presented. The leaders of the movement organized a mass meeting at Kennington, south London, designed to coincide with the petition's presentation. One of these leaders was Feargus O'Connor, who edited the Chartist newspaper the *Northern Star.* O'Connor had connections to radical organization whose leaders were prepared to engage in violence in order to achieve reform of the Parliamentary system. Military forces were held in reserve, but despite the third petition's rejection, there was no violence. By 1857 the movement had lost its influence, but there were further Reform Acts in 1867 and 1884. By 1918 five of the Chartists' original six demands had been met; the only one not achieved was Parliamentary elections every year.

drawn by his supporters. Once passed, the cavalry were ordered to stand to their horses. As the troop of the Manchester and Salford Yeomanry advanced along Cooper Street a woman and her child were knocked down and the two-year-old child killed. This was the first casualty. All eyewitnesses were in agreement that the Yeomanry's horses were not under control, emphasized in Bruton's account (p. 99):

> A mere handful of trained mounted troops properly directed, can, by feints, by backing, by rearing, and by skilful manoeuvres, break up and move a large crowd without injury to anyone. All parties are agreed that the Yeomanry halted in disorder. Even Hunt noticed that and remarked upon it, though he was a hundred yards away. On this point we have the clear testimony of the chairman of the magistrates, Mr. Hulton, who in his evidence at the trial said that 'their horses being raw, and unused to the field, they appeared to him to be in a certain degree of confusion'. Mr. Stanley, again, says, 'They halted in great disorder, and so continued for the few minutes they remained. This disorder was attributed by several persons in the room to the undisciplined state of their horses, little accustomed to act together, and probably frightened by the shout of the populace which greeted their arrival.'

Mount Street, bounded on the east by a row of houses, was the maximum extent of the crowd. There were stragglers in the spaces here, and the Yeomanry used this area to

Mount Street, looking towards Albert Square, with the Friends' Meeting House (left) and Central Library (right).

rein up as they arrived. All around St Peter's Fields, in the side streets but not visible to the protesters, were posted the regular troops and Cheshire Yeomanry, together with mounted messengers for communication between them and the magistrates' house. The question remains, would things have turned out differently if the 15th Hussars had been employed as escorts to Nadin? Hulton, the chairman of the magistrates, was emphatic in stating that their intention had been to arrest the meeting's leaders and hope that it would then disperse, as had happened with the Blanketeers two years previously. The Yeomanry now made their way slowly through the crowd, escorting the Deputy Constable towards the hustings. A woman and a special constable were killed in the confusion. Whilst the Yeomanry advanced, the 88th Infantry formed a line at Windmill Hill, preventing crowd incursions but without causing alarm. The cavalry had entered St Peter's Fields at a gallop, halting in great disorder, noted by Henry Hunt, Samuel Bamford and Bishop Stanley. Now the Yeomanry's pace increased as they progressed towards the hustings. The crowd attempted to escape, but were pressed on all sides by soldiers, special constables, the position of the hustings, and the fact that the size of the crowd made any type of manoeuvre difficult. The Yeomanry forced their way through, using their sabres to chop at hands, limbs and defenceless heads, as panic levels increased amongst the crowd.

Windmill Street and Windmill Hill from the old Midland Hotel, looking towards Deansgate.

Samuel Bamford was born on 28 February 1788, at Middleton, near Manchester. His father, Daniel, and mother, Hannah, were handloom weavers and Methodists. In the early 1790s Daniel became a radical, forming a group which met regularly at Middleton, causing conflict in the town. In 1794 the family moved to Manchester. Shortly after their arrival Samuel's mother and two brothers died of smallpox. When his father remarried, Samuel was sent to Middleton to live with his uncle, where he continued to educate himself whilst employed. On his marriage in 1812, he began working as a weaver, wrote poetry and sold books. The family, however, continued to live in poverty. He became a supporter of John Cartwright and Parliamentary reform and in 1816 formed a Middleton branch of the Hampden Reform Club. He campaigned for universal suffrage, organizing meetings in the local area, and was arrested in March 1817 for treason. He was tried in London, but was acquitted due to insufficient evidence. In 1819 he was responsible for co-ordinating the demonstrators from Middleton who attended the meeting at St Peter's Fields. His account of the Peterloo Massacre is an essential source for historians of the incident. After the massacre Bamford was arrested and sentenced to one year in Lincoln Prison. On his release he ceased to be a radical, selling poetry to make a living and becoming the Manchester correspondent for a London newspaper in 1826. He died on 13 April 1872, at Harpurhey.

The *Manchester Guardian*, reporting at the Lancaster Assizes in 1822, gives us the testimony of John Jones, a fustian cutter, of 14 Windmill Street:

Saw the cavalry come into the field. They came down towards the hustings as fast as they well could for the crowd. When they got to the hustings, they formed round them; and when they had cleared the hustings, they made a charge on the people. The people fled in all directions. The yeomanry rode over men, women and children. There was a great mass of people jammed up against his own rails. The cavalry laid on them with their swords. An officer came up and said, 'Oh, gentlemen, gentlemen; forbear; forbear. The people cannot get away.' Saw only one stone thrown, and that was when the soldiers were scouring the field. At his door there was a man killed and a woman suffocated.

Once the Yeomanry were at the hustings, speakers either fell or were forced off the scaffold. Because the hustings were raised off the ground they were out of the reach of Yeomanry swords, but Bishop Stanley saw swords going 'up and down', and could not say if they inflicted any injuries. Other accounts say that sword blades, rather than flats, were used unintentionally in the confusion of the situation. John Tyas of the *London Times* gives us an eyewitness account of events at the hustings: 'The officer who commanded the detachment went up to Mr. Hunt and said, brandishing his sword: "Sir, I have a

The *Manchester Guardian* was founded by cotton merchant John Edward Taylor (1791–1844) in 1821, two years after the Peterloo Massacre. He was financially backed by the Little Circle, a group of nonconformist businessmen. They launched the paper after the police closure of the more radical *Manchester Observer*, which had supported the cause of the Peterloo Massacre protesters. The *Manchester Observer* had published the names, addresses and occupations of those Manchester and Salford Yeomanry who had been involved in the massacre at the time of the trials on 20 April 1822. The most famous name to be associated with the newspaper is Charles Prestwich Scott (C. P. Scott 1846–1932). He was editor of the newspaper for fifty-seven years from 1872, and became its owner, buying it in 1907. The previous editorial line was moderate in tone; now it became more radical and liberal 'centre-left' even in the face of public hostility. Its reputation was enhanced both nationally and internationally. Scott supported women's suffrage, but not direct action, believing that it was detrimental to their cause. He opposed the second Boer War, against popular opinion, backed Irish independence, and supported the new state of Israel in 1948. The newspaper remained independent, with a northern and broadly nonconformist readership. The *Manchester Guardian* became *The Guardian* in 1959.

warrant against you, and arrest you as my prisoner." Mr. Hunt, after exhorting the people to tranquillity in a few words, turned round to the officer and said: "I willingly surrender myself to any civil officer who will show me his warrant." Nadin, the police officer, then came forward and said: "I will arrest you: I have got information upon oath against you." The same formality was gone through with Mr. Johnson. Mr. Hunt and Mr. Johnson then leaped from the waggon and surrendered themselves to the civil power.'

The crowd were now running in panic from the Yeomanry, who were brandishing sabres, and charging out of control. Once the Yeomanry had pushed their way through the tightly packed crowd towards the hustings, which consisted of two carts and some boards, positioned just below Windmill Street, and they got closer to their intended target, their progress was impeded by the crowd, who allegedly linked arms around the hustings in order to prevent the arrests. The Yeomanry response to this was to strike at people in the immediate vicinity with their swords and take down their banners. Hunt says that the Yeomanry charged amongst the crowd, indiscriminately cutting through them, in the direction of the hustings. Birley said he saw the crowd attacking the Yeomanry, which closed in behind the leading officers. Bishop Stanley saw no stones or missiles throughout the proceedings, although he stated that in all probability the crowd would have had to defend itself as there was no means of escape for them. However, Birley did admit that riders prioritized a charge towards the demonstrators' banners and flags. The *Manchester Chronicle* reported that other troops came to the aid of the Yeomanry – the

The old Midland Hotel and Windmill Street, looking towards Albert Square, c. 1900.

Cheshire Yeomanry, then the 15th Hussars, followed by the Royal Artillery, 'while all the various detachments of infantry also advanced'. The infantry impeded a retreat by the crowd, according to Bishop Stanley, with their appearance probably increasing the level of panic, although they took no part in the proceedings. The *London Times* reports the incident thus:

> the Yeomanry cavalry were seen advancing in a rapid trot to the area: their ranks were in disorder, and on arriving within it, they halted to breathe their horses, and to recover their ranks. A panic seemed to strike the persons at the outskirts of the meeting, who immediately began to scamper in every direction. After a moment's pause, the cavalry drew their swords, and brandished them fiercely in the air: upon which Hunt and Johnson desired the multitude to give three cheers, to show the military that they were not to be daunted in the discharge of their duty by their unwelcome presence ... As soon as Hunt and Johnson had jumped from the waggon, a cry was made by the cavalry, 'Have at their flags.' In consequence, they immediately dashed not only at the flags which were in the waggon, but those which were posted among the crowd, cutting most indiscriminately to the right and to the left in order to get at them. This set the people running in all directions, and it was not till this act had been committed that any brick-bats were hurled at the military. From that moment the Manchester Yeomanry cavalry lost all command of temper.

The 15th Hussars charging protesters on St Peter's Fields in 1819.

Around fifty to sixty Manchester and Salford Yeomanry had been surrounded by the crowd. Bruton (p. 105) gives us the testimony of Lieutenant Sir W. Jolliffe, who charged the crowd with the Hussars: 'The Manchester Yeomanry were scattered in small groups over the greater part of the field, literally hemmed up and wedged into the mob, so that they were powerless either to make an impression or to escape; in fact, they were in the power of those whom they were designed to overawe; and it required only a glance to discover their helpless position and the necessity of our being brought to the rescue.' Therefore, the ensuing panic was interpreted as the crowd attacking the Yeomanry and so the Hussars, led by Lieutenant-Colonel Guy L'Estrange, were ordered in. In the ensuing mêlée an unnamed cavalry officer attempted to strike up the swords of the Yeomanry, recognizing that the protesters had no means of escape. Samuel Bamford recalls a fierce battle raging around some timber lying in front of the Friends' Meeting House on Mount Street. The Yeomanry charged some retreating protesters, who responded by throwing stones they found lying there. This was reported in the *Manchester Chronicle*, which said, 'Another Yeomanry man was unhorsed at the same moment, and his life with difficulty saved. This was near the Quakers' meeting-house,

The Friends' Meeting House, Mount Street, was later rebuilt (1828–30) and although many of the original features are gone, the height of the existing boundary wall gives an indication of its outlook onto Mount Street.

where a furious battle raged.' The 'fragment of brick' that unseated the Yeomanry rider was thrown by a woman, whom they had already wounded, although the *Chronicle* refers to 'large stones'. (Bruton p. 106) The *Manchester Guardian*, at Lancaster Assizes, gives us the testimony of Joseph Prestwick, a weaver of Droylsden who witnessed the cavalry's activities around the Quaker's Meeting House: 'knows Alexander Oliver and Thomas Redford; Oliver he has known ten years; Redford about fifteen years. Oliver is a Manchester Yeoman; saw him in the field on 16th August; saw Redford also; saw him where he was cut, near the Quaker's Meeting-House, among some timber. Saw Oliver about 20 yards from the hustings, and afterwards saw Oliver cut Redford on the shoulder; the blow seemed to him aimed at his head: there were many other Yeoman at same time, acting in same manner. Six or seven persons accompanied him to the meeting; was stationed at first within a few yards of the hustings, and remained there till the cavalry came on at a sharp canter. He saw them wave their swords before they advanced. The meeting was peaceable and quiet. Saw no stones thrown, nor any resistance. They passed near him, making blows, and surrounded the hustings. Witness received a cut on his hand, and another on the knee. When they got to the hustings, they cleared them, and struck at some of the people; the Yeomanry then dispersed in all directions, pursuing the people. He attempted to go towards Deansgate, but could not; and then went towards where the timber lay, and there the Yeomanry were cutting. There was cavalry in different parts of the meeting. He escaped through a passage over some railings ... Sergeant Hullock. "Why did not you go towards Deansgate?" Witness. "You did not see what I saw, or you would not ask such a question."' Although this testimony was given three years after the event, it corroborates other evidence, which stated that the Yeomanry were charging out of control and intent on causing as much harm as was possible, both within the confines of St Peter's Fields and beyond.

An important question is: Was the Riot Act read before the second wave of troops was deployed? According to the trial of 1822 it was read twice, but no one close enough, or relevant to its reading, heard or saw it read. If it was read, the required one hour between the Riot Act's reading and the charge of the troops was not adhered to. The *London Times* picks up on this important point:

> The Riot Act and the act against seditious meetings, both limit the magistrate's right of interference, to 'unlawful assemblies,' and no other. Was that at Manchester an 'unlawful assembly?' Was the notice of it unlawful? We believe not. Was the subject proposed for discussion (a reform in the House of Commons) an unlawful subject? Assuredly not. Was anything done at this meeting before the cavalry rode in upon it, either contrary to law or in breach of the peace? No such circumstance is recorded in any of the statements which have yet reached our hand ... The Riot Act, some say, was read; some say otherwise – but all are agreed, that before an hour had elapsed from the reading of it, the soldiers attacked, and the people were cut down.

There were many representatives of the press present at the demonstration, including John Tyas of the *London Times*. However, few had as privileged a position as he did on the hustings, close to Henry Hunt and able to hear clearly all that transpired on the build-up to the speakers' arrest. Tyas's report is by far the most complete and detailed of all the contemporary Peterloo press reports, essentially because of his place at the demonstration, and so it is quoted in detail here as part of the record:

> MR. TYAS went down from London to take notes of whatever he should see and hear, and report it for *The Times*. He is a gentleman of talent and education; nephew to an individual of great respectability in the town of Manchester, and, so far as we can judge from his preceding conduct towards this journal, about as much a Jacobin, or friend of Jacobins, as is Lord LIVERPOOL himself. MR. TYAS has been very seriously indisposed from the day of his arrival at Manchester. Anxious, however, to discharge, in the most satisfactory manner, his duty to us and to the public, he determined to procure, if possible, a place near HUNT on the day of the meeting, for the sake of sparing his own infirm health, and for the greater facility of sending us a complete report. By what means he so unluckily succeeded in this purpose, as to be considered one of HUNT's party, we have yet no materials for conjecturing: but, greatly as we have been grieved for his sake by this accident, and severely as it has disappointed our hopes of affording more ample and perfect information to our readers, we mention the circumstances less as a subject of complaint with regard to our personal feelings, than as a mode of illustrating the manner in which those who acted for the magistrates thought fit to exercise the power, and to discharge the functions assigned to them. MR. TYAS, we have reason to know, was absolutely unacquainted with HUNT, at the moment of his entering Manchester: of what has since happened, we are as ignorant as the public at large.

Once the Yeomanry had charged into the crowd and started to wield their sabres, Tyas, who was positioned on the hustings, recalls what happened as they tried to make their escape in the aftermath of the massacre: 'looking around us we saw a constable at no great distance, and thinking that our only chance of safety rested in placing ourselves under his protection, we appealed to him for assistance. He immediately took us into custody, and on our saying that we merely attended to report the proceedings of the day, he replied, "Oh! Oh! You then are one of their writers. You must go before the Magistrates." To this we made no objection: in consequence he took us to the house where they were sitting, and in our road thither, we saw a woman on the ground, insensible, to all outward appearance, and with two large gouts of blood on her left breast. Just as we came to the house, the constables were conducting Hunt into it, and were treating him in a manner in which they were neither justified by law nor humanity, striking him with their staves on the head. After he had been taken into the house, we were admitted also; and it is only justice to the man that apprehended us to state, that he did everything in his power to protect us from ill-usage, and showed us every civility consistent with his duty.'

Hunt was consigned to the custody of Colonel L'Estrange of the 31st Foot and a detachment of the 15th Hussars, and under his care he and all the other prisoners, who were each placed between two constables, reached the New Bailey in perfect safety. The staffs of two of Hunt's banners were carried in mock procession before him. The writer of this article was one of the parties thus imprisoned. Except for his sentence, he has no reason to complain of the treatment which he received:

He was in custody from 2 o'clock on Monday, till 12 o'clock on Tuesday. As soon as the magistrates were acquainted with the circumstances under which his apprehension had taken place, they immediately ordered his release, and expressed in very polite terms their regret for the inconvenience to which he had been subjected. When we were once more allowed to enjoy that freedom of which we had been for a moment deprived, we took a walk through most of the principal streets of Manchester, and found that they were at that time (12 o'clock) completely under military disposal. Soldiers were posted at all the commanding positions of the town, and were to be seen extended at full length on the flags in various directions. At three o' clock, they had, however, all of them returned to their quarters, and the town was to all outward appearance once more in a state of tranquillity. At seven o' clock, when we quitted Manchester, all was quiet in the town. A report had, however, reached it that there was a serious riot at Oldham, and in consequence some troops of the Chester Yeomanry were sent to quell it.

A report in the *Manchester Guardian* tells us about the trial which took place at Lancaster in 1822, where John Tyas was cross-examined:

John Tyas furnished a report for the *Times* London Journal, was at Manchester for the purpose on the 16th was at the field as early as 8 o'clock; was to and fro. About half past eleven saw two bodies of reformers come on the ground with two banners, each surmounted by a cap of liberty; they were peaceable and quiet. Witness went away; when he returned between twelve and one, there were many persons assembled. Being unwell he applied to Mr. Hunt, and was enabled to get on the hustings; at that time the meeting was cheering Mr. Hunt, who made a speech from five to ten minutes long. Saw the Yeomanry cavalry advancing, rapidly to the area where the meeting was held; they formed opposite to Buxton's; could not then distinguish constables from the people – did afterwards by seeing their truncheons. Observed the cavalry advance to the hustings. The people were closely jammed together round the hustings: the people up to the advance of the cavalry were orderly in the extreme. Has attended many other meetings. When the cavalry advanced the people gave way in every direction as fast as they could before them; the cavalry advanced rapidly at first but they could not get on quick for the mass of people. Was on the hustings to the time of their arrival: saw no stones or sticks thrown. It was impossible for him to see arms locked below the hustings, unless in front; did not see any there. On the advance heard nothing said: after Hunt was taken, heard a cry of 'have at the flags.' Immediately after, the Yeomanry began cutting at them: saw several persons on the ground bleeding. Does not know Oliver, nor any of the Yeomanry by name, knows one by sight ... was taken and detained twenty hours in custody.

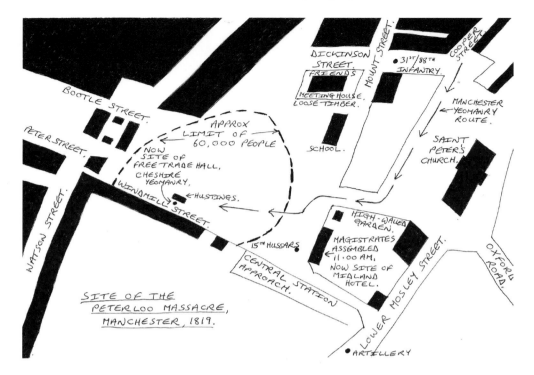

Map of the site of St Peter's Fields and the Peterloo Massacre, Manchester, in 1819.

Lieutenant-Colonel L'Estrange arrived on Windmill Street with the 15th Hussars and the Cheshire Yeomanry, where he communicated with the magistrates, asking 'What am I to do?' Hulton, the chairman of the magistrates, replied that more military were to go in. Although he did not directly consult his fellow magistrates, they were present and close enough to hear the proceedings. Hulton replied, 'Good God sir; don't you see they are attacking the Yeomanry? Disperse the meeting.' From this exchange it took ten minutes to clear St Peter's Fields, the assembled demonstrators fleeing in blind panic and confusion. Bruton (p. 110) quotes Wheeler's *Manchester Chronicle*, which he describes as 'the principal Tory organ', to give us a vivid description of the aftermath of the 15th Hussars charge into the demonstrators:

A scene of confusion and terror now existed which defies description. The multitude pressed one another down, and in many places they lay in masses, piled body upon body. The cries and mingled shouts with the galloping of the horses were shocking. Many of the most respectable gentlemen of the town were thrown down, ridden over, and trampled upon. One special constable was killed on the spot; another was borne home dreadfully hurt. The whole of this serious affray lasted not many minutes. The ground was cleared as if by magic.

Lieutenant Jolliffe gives an account of the conclusion of fighting at the Friends' Meeting House: 'The mob had taken possession of various buildings, particularly of a Quakers' chapel and burial-ground enclosed with a wall. This they occupied for some little time, and in attempting to displace them some of the men and horses were struck with stones and brickbats. Seeing a sort of fighting going on, I went in that direction. At the very moment I reached the Quakers' meeting-house, I saw a farrier of the 15th ride at a small door in the outer wall, and to my surprise his horse struck it with such force that it flew open. Two or three Hussars then rode in, and the place was immediately in their possession.' (Bruton p. 111)

Gunshots were fired from a nearby rooftop, but the perpetrators were cleared from the area by the 88th Infantry. The vast majority of the infantry were held in reserve, as were the Cheshire Yeomanry. Both allowed passage for the retreating demonstrators as they fled from the 15th Hussars. Despite their hurried withdrawal, many of the demonstrators were bent on revenge. The *London Times* reports on the centre of the disaffection, at New Cross, where the Riot Act was read, and several people were wounded, one fatally, by gunfire from the military:

New Cross, the place where the most dangerous rioting had occurred on Monday evening, was taken possession of during the morning of Tuesday, by companies of the 31st regiment of foot, who relieved each other in succession. An attempt was made by the very lowest of the populace to assemble there at the early hour of seven, but they were soon put to flight, and by nine o'clock everything was tranquil in that quarter ... A report (which appears to have been spread with the view of diverting the attention of the military) was circulated early in the morning, that a large body of the disaffected, armed with pikes, amounting in number to 15,000, were advancing to Manchester by the Oldham road. A party of the 15th Light Dragoons, with two pieces of artillery, were immediately stationed in Oldham street; and the Cheshire Yeomanry, who were previously on duty at St. Peter's green, were ordered to advance on the road to Oldham. This alarm proving to be unfounded, the troops and artillery were withdrawn by two 'clock ... Manchester Mercury, 7 o'clock:- 'The Riot Act has just been read at the New Cross in consequence of the windows of Mr. Tate, grocer, being entirely demolished by stones from the pavement. The town certainly wears an alarming aspect at the present moment; but we are well supplied with military protection, and their exertions and resolute conduct are truly praiseworthy, and a theme of general eulogium.'

The immediate aftermath of the Peterloo Massacre saw repeated requests and refusals for an enquiry into the incident. Henry Hunt was imprisoned and on his release he was triumphantly borne to Manchester and then received by an enormous crowd in London. There were discussions as to the legality of the meeting and the right of the magistrates to interfere. A Relief Committee investigated around 600 cases of those killed and wounded at the demonstration and a 'test trial' of Thomas Redford at Lancaster in 1822 was dismissed after six minutes of deliberation. However, their efforts sowed the

Thomas Barnes, the editor of the *London Times*, was understandably angry that John Tyas, one of his journalists, had been arrested at the Peterloo meeting. Tyas was unable to send his report, so The *Times* published a piece written by John Edward Taylor, who worked for the *Manchester Gazette*. Neither Tyas or Taylor were considered radicals, but Taylor was angered by events surrounding the massacre perpetrated by his fellow Mancunians; therefore his report was very critical of the authorities' treatment of the Reformers and their organization of the demonstration. Tyas's full account was published on the 19 August, after his release, and is referenced in this chapter. The *Times* subsequently campaigned against the magistrates' actions at St Peter's Fields. As an establishment newspaper, any criticism of official actions by The *Times* was particularly damaging.

seeds of liberty. What had started out as a call for Parliamentary representation became a mass movement for the cause of radicalism. Peterloo's legacy saw the Corn Laws repealed some twenty years after the massacre. Parliamentary representation soon followed, and local government on the basis of the ballot box and one man one vote, swept away the antiquated manorial courts. Manchester Corporation was established, the old market town was given city status as the economy and population boomed, and by the time that Bruton's work was published in 1921 women had the vote. Bruton (p. 116) quotes Richard Cobden's pamphlet *Incorporate Your Borough*, issued to the people of Manchester in 1838: 'Peterloo could never have happened if the Borough had been incorporated. Why? Because the magistrates of Lancashire and Cheshire, who entered the town and sat at the Star Inn to take command of the police, and order the soldiers to cut down and trample upon unarmed crowds, would have no more jurisdiction over Manchester than Constantinople.' The radical demonstrators of Peterloo left a long-term legacy of political freedom to the working class of the British Isles, which we still enjoy today.

And what of the short-lived influence of the Manchester and Salford Yeomanry? The *Manchester Guardian* reports on the St George's Day celebrations of 1822:

An attempt was made by some of the persons in the centre of the square, to raise a cheer for the Yeomanry as they left the ground; but it so completely failed as to be scarcely even perceptible to those who stood upon the flags. The most efficient cheerers were a few of the Yeomanry themselves, who waved their swords *a-la-mode de* Peterloo, and shouted as loud as they could from the same principle, we suppose, as that on which men sometimes drink their own healths.

Their respect amongst the Mancunian public continued to decline until they were disbanded in 1824.

4. THE BOER WAR OF 1899 TO 1902, THE GREAT WAR OF 1914 TO 1918, AND THE LEGACY OF THE MANCHESTER REGIMENT

The Manchester Regiment, 1881–1918

The Manchester Regiment has seen service all over the world, including Egypt, Guadeloupe, Afghanistan, South Africa, France and Flanders, Mesopotamia, Malta, Malaya, Burma and India. The regiment was formed as a result of the implementation of reforms by Edward Cardwell and Hugh Childers. It came into being on 1 July 1881 by the union of the 63rd (West Suffolk) and 96th Regiment of Foot. They had previously been associated by their allocation to the 16th Sub-District Brigade Depot at Ashton-under-Lyne, Manchester. The 2nd Battalion, as the 96th Foot, had been raised in Manchester in 1824. The 1st Battalion were sent to Egypt in 1882 as part of the Anglo-Egyptian war and then in 1897 to Gibraltar. In the same time period the 2nd Battalion were based in India and saw service on the North-West Frontier before they were deployed to Aden.

The Boer War was a formidable test for the British Army as the Boers were skilled and committed fighters, both in conventional battle and in guerrilla tactics, at which they were specialists. The 1st Manchesters set out for South Africa in September 1899, with the battalion arriving in Durban, Natal Colony, in early October. On their arrival they were very quickly moved down the line to Ladysmith, with the war beginning on 11 October when the Boers invaded the colony. After the Boers had captured the railway station at Elandslaagte, the Manchesters sent four companies by armoured train to Modderspruit. Whilst at the station they came under artillery fire, together with the Imperial Light Horse who were travelling with them. Fortunately, there were no casualties on this occasion.

The 1st Manchesters, the Imperial Light Horse and the Gordon Highlanders now advanced upon the Boers, whose accurate and heavy fire forced the British advance to halt. However, the 1st Manchesters continued with a frontal assault, which pushed the Boers back to their main line of defence. On 2 November 1899 the Boers encircled and besieged Ladysmith, an action that lasted 118 days. Clearly in the ascendancy, on 6 January 1900, the Boers attacked sixteen soldiers of the 1st Manchesters at Waggon Hill, near Caesar's Camp. However, the British held out for fifteen hours, with only two survivors – Privates James Pitts and Robert Scott – who both received the Victoria Cross for their actions. These were the first for the regiment. On 28 February 1900 Ladysmith was finally relieved – by a force under the command of General Redvers Buller – concluding the first major action of the campaign.

In April, the 2nd Manchesters arrived in Natal as reinforcements, with both battalions taking part in the offensive that followed the relief of Ladysmith, Kimberley and

The 1st Manchesters at The Point, Durban, Natal Colony, in October 1899, on their way to the front.

A Boer commando poses in front of Spion Kop. As guerrillla fighters, the Manchesters found the Boers formidable opponents. (Photo Project Gutenberg)

Mafeking. After the fall of Bloemfontein and Pretoria, the Boer commandos increasingly made use of guerrilla warfare tactics. This meant that the 2nd Manchesters were participating in a style of warfare with which they were not familiar. They operated in the Orange Free State, engaged in searching farms and burning those who were believed to be harbouring Boer guerrillas. These actions led to the decimation of the agricultural infrastructure and the use of concentration camps in order to round up dissident populations sympathetic to the Boer commandos and their use of guerrilla warfare. This ultimately led to their displacement and created a logistical difficulty at the campaign's conclusion, as reported in the *Manchester Guardian*. The war was brought to an end with the signing of the Treaty of Vereeniging in May 1902. The *Manchester Guardian,* in June 1902, reports in detail the terms and aftermath of the signing of the treaty:

> Owing to the protracted nature of the peace negotiations and the uncertainty of the result until the last moment, the emotions of the inhabitants of Pretoria had been so keenly excited that the announcement of peace when it came was received with comparative calm. Reference to the auspicious event was made from the pulpits of most of the churches in the town, and in some cases thanksgiving services were held, all breathing the same spirit of deep thankfulness that the end of the war had come.

Manchesters on Waggon Hill. (Photo courtesy of Joanna Neal via Gerry van Tonder)

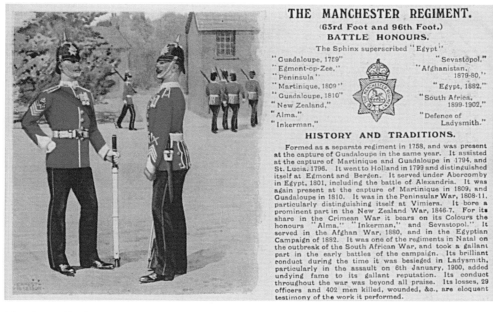

THE MANCHESTER REGIMENT.
(63rd Foot and 96th Foot.)
BATTLE HONOURS.

The Sphinx superscribed "Egypt"

"Guadaloupe, 1759"	"Sevastopol."
"Egmont-op-Zee."	"Afghanistan, 1879-80,"
"Peninsula"	
"Martinique, 1809"	"Egypt, 1882,"
"Guadaloupe, 1810"	"South Africa, 1899-1902,"
"New Zealand,"	
"Alma,"	"Defence of
"Inkerman."	Ladysmith."

HISTORY AND TRADITIONS.

Formed as a separate regiment in 1758, and was present at the capture of Guadaloupe in the same year. It assisted at the capture of Martinique and Guadaloupe in 1794, and St. Lucia, 1796. It went to Holland in 1799 and distinguished itself at Egmont and Bergen. It served under Abercomby in Egypt, 1801, including the battle of Alexandria. It was again present at the capture of Martinique in 1809, and Guadaloupe in 1810. It was in the Peninsular War, 1808-11, particularly distinguishing itself at Vimiera. It bore a prominent part in the New Zealand War, 1846-7. For its share in the Crimean War it bears on its Colours the honours "Alma," "Inkerman," and "Sevastopol." It served in the Afghan War, 1880, and in the Egyptian Campaign of 1882. It was one of the regiments in Natal on the outbreak of the South African War, and took a gallant part in the early battles of the campaign. Its brilliant conduct during the time it was besieged in Ladysmith, particularly in the assault on 6th January, 1900, added undying fame to its gallant reputation. Its conduct throughout the war was beyond all praise. Its losses, 29 officers and 402 men killed, wounded, &c., are eloquent testimony of the work it performed.

Manchester Regiment, 1912.

The Boer delegates, usually phlegmatic, took no pains to hide their joy at the termination of hostilities. Throughout yesterday morning they collected at Gordon House, laughing, chatting and showing their satisfaction in every way. General Botha remarked that it was the happiest day he had known since he left school. The Boer population of the town also showed every sign of joy at the result of the negotiations.

The only step now remaining is to bring in the commandos which are still in the field. The delegates will proceed by special trains to the different points in order to bring in their several commandos. It appears that no difficulty is anticipated in the accomplishment of this task. A full return is prepared as the prisoners surrender showing the domicile of each and his nearest destination on the railway. The arrangements for their transport have been in preparation for some time and are already well advanced.

The work of returning the wives and children as well as the men to their farms will be enormous. It is impossible to send them straight back, as it is absolutely necessary at this time of the year to have warm shelters ready for them. To meet this difficulty wooden huts have already been ordered at the coast, to be delivered in sections, for each family. The conditions upon which the owners of farms shall be resettled upon them have already received careful consideration on the part of the authorities. It is expected that if the former proprietors desire it they will be allowed to return to their old habitations, but those who are unable to resume farming operations on the old conditions will be temporarily supported in some manner by the Government. The question of restocking the denuded farms is also in hand, the great difficulty being to ascertain what kind of exported cattle would be likely to thrive upon them. In regard to horses, no serious difficulty is anticipated, at least for the present, since the cessation of hostilities will enable the Government to sell to the population a great number of remounts. With respect to the cattle which have been brought in, they must be sent to the fresh veld, as this is the only place where they will be able to subsist through the winter. The various Government farms however ... will be able to support a fair number of cattle during the winter ...

Although at the present moment the excitement aroused by the termination of the war leads people to indulge in somewhat emotional expressions, yet apart from these there are hopeful signs as to the possibility of concord in the future. One of these is the fact that the British population has shown no undue exultation at this juncture. I had a conversation yesterday with an ardent young Boer, who has played a considerable part in the war. He quoted the words of Mr. Kruger when he said, "If the Transvaal is to be conquered we would prefer England as our master rather than any other nation in the world." The young man in question expressed his firm conviction that the Boers would in the end become loyal British subjects, and concluded the conversation by drinking to the health of his British brothers. The formal recognition of the altered state of affairs produced by peace is to take the excellent form of a public thanksgiving service, to be held in the church square next Sunday at ten o'clock, when 2,000 troops will parade. The fact that it is a thanksgiving service for peace will allow our late foes to take part in the ceremony without bitterness ...

The question of the concentration camps, which is also under Lord Milner's jurisdiction, is receiving his earnest attention. Many of the women are anxious to return to their homes at once, but of course until a proper system of supply depots has been established in the outlying districts it is impossible to allow them to return ...

All the signs throughout the Rand show the joy of the people at the conclusion of hostilities. The satisfaction felt is expressed everywhere. Flags are flying, and thanksgiving services have been arranged. Everyone rejoices at the conclusion of peace with honour. In fact, the sense of hope so long deferred has now given place to one of rest and a feeling of relief and gratification at the full reality of becoming subjects of King Edward.

The Union Jack has been hoisted over the burgher concentration camp, and the inmates have shown their appreciation of the situation by hoisting white flags over their tents ... The Commander-in-Chief, after his address to the delegates, returned to Pretoria, and the work of sending the delegates to the different districts to carry the glad tidings of peace to the burghers still in the field commenced. The trains conveying the delegates were not despatched until late, and the night being extremely cold huge bonfires were lighted by the sentries along the railway track, and around each of these groups of Boers and Britons collected and fraternised. The scene for some miles out of Vereeniging was highly picturesque, and the enthusiasm of both sides was great. Boers joined with Britons in singing patriotic songs at more than one big bonfire ... the 'Tommies' and the burghers out-vying each other in their demonstrations of joy.

Back home in Britain there were similar 'demonstrations of joy'. At Sale an ox roast was organized for the townspeople. In a photograph of 1902 the ox is shown being paraded through the streets of the town, where it is passing the Waggon and Horses public house on Cross Street (Chester Road) to much acclaim. Many areas of Manchester honoured the South African campaign by naming streets after significant battles and sieges, such as Ladysmith, Mafeking and (well known to football fans) Spion Kop.

At the beginning of the First World War the 1st Manchesters were based in India, whilst the 2nd Manchesters returned to Britain in 1902 and stayed until the outbreak of war in 1914. The 1st Manchesters left South Africa and headed for Singapore in 1903, moving to India in 1904. In 1911 the battalion paraded at the Delhi Durbar before King George V and Queen Mary, and in September 1914 they landed at Marseilles, reaching the front on 26 October 1914. The 2nd Manchesters left for France in August 1914 and assisted the British Expeditionary Force in their retreat from the Battle of Mons. On 29 October 1914 a German attack led to the retaking of a trench by a platoon led by Second Lieutenant James Leach. The action saw eight killed, two wounded and fourteen captured. Leach and Sergeant John Hogan were both awarded Victoria Crosses. Other actions involving the regiment included the Battle of Neuve Chapelle, where the 1st Manchesters suffered severe casualties. There were also casualties from the Marne, Aisne, the First Battle of Ypres, the Second Battle of Ypres and the Battle of Loos.

The Waggon and Horses Public House, Cross Street, Chester Road, Sale, 1902. Many localities across the country held an ox roast like this one at Sale to celebrate the end of the Boer War.

Field Marshal Douglas Haig is best remembered for his involvement at the Battle of the Somme. He was born in Edinburgh in 1861 and was commissioned into the cavalry in 1885, serving in the Sudan and the Boer War of 1899–1902. In August 1914 Haig was general commanding the First Army Corps, serving at Mons and 'First' Ypres. In December 1915, he became the commander-in-chief of the British Army at the Western Front. However, he was slow to embrace new military ideas and continued with conventional tactics, being criticized for refusing to reverse them at the Somme, despite huge losses. The use of a rolling artillery barrage against the German defences failed to take into account the fact that the Germans were much more effectively dug in than the British anticipated. Once the artillery barrage stopped it was as good as a direct signal to the German lines that the British infantry were on their way. The tank was first used extensively at the Somme, but this was a tactic not supported by Haig, or other senior cavalry officers, who preferred more traditional methods of warfare, which resulted in small land gains for massive loss of life. Haig served until the end of the war and was created an earl in 1919. He supported ex-servicemen disabled in the war, the 'Poppy Day' Appeal and the British Legion movement. He died in 1928.

Commander-in-Chief Douglas Haig in 1915.

A company of 1st Manchesters on the march, Lestrem, France, 1915. (Photo H. D. Girdwood)

The Manchester Regiment captures the village of Givenchy in December 1914.

Popular weapons used by the British Army in the First World War included the Lee-Enfield rifle. It was a small-bore bolt-action rifle that fired multiple rounds from a spring-loaded clip inserted into the magazine. The Lee-Enfield was introduced in 1907 and by the start of the First World War was the British Army's main infantry weapon. It was estimated that the highly trained British Expeditionary Force, on their arrival in France in September 1914, could fire fifteen rounds per minute. The Lee-Enfield could be aimed accurately over approximately 600 metres, but was still effective up to around 1,400 metres. The Vickers gun was adopted by the British Army as its standard machine gun in 1912. It was a modified version of the Maxim machine gun. The Vickers used a 250-round fabric belt magazine and had the reputation of being a highly reliable weapon. There were usually six men in a Vickers gun team and although they were all assigned different tasks, they were all trained in handling the gun. The Lewis gun was a light machine gun developed in the United States in 1911. At 12 kilograms it was far lighter than the Vickers. In 1915 the British Army decided to purchase the gun for use on the Western Front. It was too heavy to be carried over an effective distance, especially rough terrain, but became the standard support weapon for the British Infantry during the First World War.

The Manchester Regiment were again very quickly at the forefront of the action. One afternoon towards the end of December 1914, at approximately 1600 hours, they scored an impressive success at the little village of Givenchy, located on rising ground near La Bassée. It was the scene of some very furious fighting. The village was in the possession of the Germans but was captured by the regiment, which then drove the enemy back to fresh positions beyond. The Germans had dug trenches and prepared shelters in the gardens of the houses throughout the village. The fighting went on from defensive position to defensive position. House after house and wall after wall were captured by the advancing Manchester Regiment. The defenders were always losing ground but managed to keep at an average distance of around 20 yards from the advancing Manchester Regiment. The Germans were eventually driven back from the village, put to flight and the position now taken by the British. Many of the Manchester Regiment who fell at Givenchy were discovered between the ruined walls of what had once been houses.

On the first day of the Battle of the Somme the regiment had nine battalions deployed, which included the Manchester 'Pals', the 16th (First City), 17th (Second City), 18th (Third City), and 19th (Fourth City), all serving in the 90th Brigade of the 30th Division. By the end of the day there were more than 57,000 killed, wounded, or missing. It was the most disastrous day in the British Army's history thus far. The *Manchester Evening News* reports on the first casualty of the Pals battalions in November 1915:

The first casualty among the Manchester Pals Battalions is announced to-day, the parents of Second-Lieutenant A. E. Townsend having received official intimation that he

Two soldiers of the 5th Battalion, Manchester Regiment buying apples from a woman near the front at Cambrin. (Photo John Warwick Boothe via IWM)

has died of wounds received in France. Lieutenant Townsend, who was 27 years of age, lived with his parents in Lansdowne Road, West Didsbury, and was an officer in the 18th (Service) Battalion Manchester Regiment.

He had been for years in a Manchester Territorial Battalion, and at the outbreak of war he again endeavoured to join the Territorials, but owing to the fact that he had just undergone an operation for varicose veins he was not passed. He got all right again, and at once joined the "Pals." Before being given his commission he had occupied all ranks as a non-commissioned officer. His brother, J. E. Townsend, is a Captain in the 22nd (Service) Battalion Manchester Regiment. In business the unfortunate officer was engaged at the Alliance Assurance Company, King Street, Manchester. Only last Tuesday his parents received a letter from him stating that he was alright.

Further loss of life and acts of heroism continued until the Somme offensive. In late July the 16th 17th and 18th battalions of the Manchester Regiment attacked an area close to the village of Guillemont. During this action Company Sergeant-Major George Evans, of the 18th Battalion, volunteered to deliver a vital message, despite the five previous attempts to deliver it proving fatal for the individual concerned. Company Sergeant-Major George Evans successfully delivered the message, running more than

Recuperating Soldiers at Basford House Auxillary Hospital, Seymour Grove, Old Trafford, later in the war.

The Battle of the Somme, 1 July 1916–November 1916, became the battle that symbolized the horror and futility of trench warfare. Casualty figures peaked around the one million mark. Douglas Haig, the commander of the British campaign, was severely criticized for his leadership on the basis of these figures, which were 420,000 for the British, with 60,000 on the first day; 200,000 for the French; and nearly 500,000 for the Germans. For many, the Somme was their first and only experience of battle. They were part of Kitchener's 'volunteer army', with no concept of what real war entailed or the terrors of trench warfare. The British volunteer was not trained, nor prepared, for life on the battlefield. The Somme's aim was to relieve the French, who had been taking severe losses at Verdun, east of Paris. In order to achieve this it was decided to mount an attack to the north of Verdun, therefore forcing the Germans to redeploy their forces away from this area. The battle started with a week-long artillery bombardment of the German lines – 1,738,000 shells were fired – in an attempt to break through across a 25-mile front, thus allowing an infantry advance. There were even plans to utilize cavalry! The Germans, sheltered in deep dugouts, used their machine guns on advancing infantry once the bombardment had stopped. The Allies gained a 30-mile strip, 7 miles deep at its maximum.

Former Manchester Grammar School teacher Lieutenant William Thomas Forshaw was awarded a Victoria Cross for gallantry, in the Middle East Campaign of 1915. *Inset*: Sergeant John Hogan VC.

half a mile despite being wounded. For this action he was awarded the Victoria Cross. Further actions by the Manchester Regiment at Francilly-Selency, on 2 April 1917, saw C Company capture guns. They fought in the Arras offensive, and at Messines the Manchester Pals fought in the opening battle (Third Ypres) at Pilckem Ridge, on 31 July. Third Ypres (Passchendale) saw Sergeant Coverdale of the 11th (Service) Battalion kill three snipers, charge two machine-gun positions and take charge of his platoon to capture another position.

On 21 March 1918 the 16th Battalion occupied positions in an area known as Manchester Hill, near St Quentin. A large German force attacked along a broad front, eventually completely encircling the 16th Battalion. Commanded by Lieutenant-Colonel Wilfrith Elstob, the 16th Battalion resolutely dug in and defended their positions. Elstob repulsed a grenade attack and replenished ammunition supplies. His messages to 42nd Brigade Headquarters and the men under his command tell us of their steadfast determination: 'The Manchester Regiment will defend Manchester Hill to the last,' and 'Here we fight and here we die.' The 16th Battalion Manchester Regiment were wiped out and Elstob was awarded a posthumous Victoria Cross for his heroic actions. The 17th Battalion (now part of 21st Brigade) attempted to retake the hill, with yet more heavy losses. Two more Victoria Crosses were gained by the regiment before the end of the war. A further Victoria Cross was awarded in the Middle East campaign, during the third Battle of Krithia, on 4 June 1915, at the Battle of Krithia Vineyard. Lieutenant Forshaw of the 9th Battalion

Manchester Regiment working party, Ancre, January 1917. (IWM)

earned a Victoria Cross for gallantry. The Manchester Regiment were also involved in the Mesopotamia campaign. At the Battle of Dujaila, in March 1916, Private Stringer defended the flank of his battalion and was awarded the Victoria Cross for his actions.

However, it was the Battle of the Somme which became synonymous with mass slaughter, and there are many of us today who know of relatives that gave their lives in this campaign, including my great-grandfather Thomas's nephew, Charles Henry Dickens (Dickins), who was killed in action aged twenty-eight. He was born in Ashton on Mersey in 1887, the eldest son of George Barker and Sarah Dickens (née Derbyshire) and, like his father, was employed as a plumber. He was also an excellent runner with both Sale and Salford Harriers. Charles was a private (No. 15405) with the 8th Battalion King's Own (Royal Lancaster Regiment). The 8th Battalion were attached to the 76th Brigade, 3rd Division, during the Battle of the Somme. They did not take part in the first day of the campaign. On 1 July they entrained at St Omer for Doullens and from there marched to Autheux. On 3 July they marched to Naors; on 4 July to Coisy; on 5 July to Franvillers; on 6 July to Celestines Wood; on 8 July to Bronfay Farm; on 13 July to Carnoy; and on 14 July to Caterpillar Wood. They were in support of the 1st Battalion Gordon Highlanders during operations at Longueval and Delville Wood on 18 July. They were relieved and moved to Bund Trench, near Carnoy, on 19 July and then to trenches south-west of Longueval on 22 July. On 23 July they withdrew back to Bund Trench, and then to Montauban Alley on 24 July. A Company were sent forward in support at Delville Wood and were relieved on 25 July, via Bund Trench, to Bois des Tailles, and then Mericourt on 28 July.

On 11 August they moved to Sandpit Camp, then Talus Boise on 14 August. On 16 August, at 1740 hours, they attacked Lonely Trench. The War Diary tells us that there

Emblem of the King's Own (Royal Lancaster Regiment).

were heavy casualties as a result of machine-gun fire and rifle fire as soon as the assault was launched. Renewed attacks met with a similar result, with all the officers and NCOs of B and C companies becoming casualties. The total number of casualties from the period 16–18 August was 271. Charles Henry Dickens was killed at Lonely Trench, which was situated just to the north of Fricourt. He and his comrades had been in France for around five weeks, in transit for much of the time, and this was the battalion's first serious action. Charles was a regular worshipper at Sale Wesleyan Chapel, but their war memorial lists a C. F. Dickens (possibly a misspelling re- the initial 'F'). However, on the town war memorial at Sale town hall he is listed as C. H. Dickins, an alternative surname spelling common throughout my family. St Martin's parish church war memorial at Ashton on Mersey also lists him, as does its memorial window. On 8 December 1916 he is listed in the local newspaper, but is not confirmed as dead until 11 May 1917. However, the Guardian Year Book Roll of Honour lists him for 1918. Charles is also honoured on the Thiepval Memorial in France. Charles had two brothers serving. George Barker Junior was a sergeant in the Royal Lancaster Regiment (No. 15297) and John Heywood was a private with the 12th Battalion, Machine Gun Corps (No. 86063). John's

Commonwealth cemetery at the Somme, viewed from across the French countryside.

war office record tells us that he attested on the 1 October 1915 and was called up on 24 May 1916. He was drafted to France on 21 April 1917 and returned via Dieppe on 29 January 1919. (www.traffordwardead.co.uk)

The war stories and records of these members of my family are not unusual, and indeed are probably fairly typical, comparable to thousands of other contemporary First World War records. Their conscription was part of a concerted effort by the British Army to increase the number of recruits to the front line. These efforts are extensively reported in the local press, including the *Manchester Evening News*. The Manchester Regiment and the Pals battalions are given particular attention. There were four battalions of the Manchester Regiment at Heaton Park by early 1915, but none had, as of yet, recruited enough men for the formation of the extra company to cross to France with the existing battalions. However, the 17th Battalion, commanded by Colonel A. H. Johnson intended to aim higher than the 1,300 required, by raising an extra company to act as a feeder for the battalion when it went on service.

The 17th Battalion opened a recruiting office at the Market Street end of Spring Gardens, with a doctor and attesting staff in situ. Men of the battalion were also brought into Manchester in an effort to target likely recruits to the regiment from Manchester's streets. The newspapers reported on the battalions' visits to the Theatre Royal pantomime and emphasized the fact that every evening a five-minute recruiting appeal would be delivered from the stage. One can only imagine the level of patriotism raised by attendance at these interval recruitment sessions. Manchester Corporation also played its part by providing special tramcars to and from the event. Route marches were also staged in order to drum up enthusiasm for recruitment, terminating and reassembling in Albert Square for the march back after a two-hour recruitment campaign. Further inducements were offered by the issuing of new uniform and equipment to the battalions. However, according to the *Manchester Evening News* in February 1915, 'Delays ... may be unavoidable in some cases, as it has been found that the old measurements are of no use. Almost without exception the men have grown broader and taller during the five months they have been in training, and the "small sizes" have all had to be returned to stores.'

It was claimed that the open-air life, early rising and regular exercise had contributed to this improvement. As a further inducement to the prospective recruit it was also claimed that the close comradeship developed during training added to the overall mental and physical health of the men, as did the excellent diet. The battalion suggested that it was the 'best fed in the North of England'. The battalion also maintained the pressure for recruitment by visiting some of the Manchester warehouses. According to the *Manchester Evening News* they were looking to recruit from 150 to 400, so that when they were required to move they would have all the men they needed. By the following week Manchester was breaking all recruiting records. The 17th Manchesters, based at Heaton Park, was the first of the 'City' battalions to make full numbers for its extra companies. Three-figure recruitment as a daily average had been maintained for a few months before this report was published and it would appear that the push to continue

Heaton Park Camp in 1914.

recruiting was well and truly on in Manchester. On 15 February 1915 the 17th Battalion recruited around forty men at their new office in Spring Gardens, a situation which they hoped to continue into the following day with the arrival of the 1,100-strong 17th Battalion in Albert Square.

The recruiting route march from Heaton Park to the city centre must have been quite a spectacle, as all the recruits (with a few exceptions) were now in their full khaki uniforms. The 17th Battalion marched into Albert Square to the strains of the R.F.A. band and with the Lord Mayor (Alderman McCabe) and other members of Manchester Corporation present, standing on the town hall steps. As the men marched through Swann Street, crowds of people thronged the pavements and hung out of upper-floor windows in order to gain a better view. Those same crowds of thousands followed the men into Albert Square, cheering wildly as they went. Colonel H. A. Johnson was in command, the other mounted officers being Major Corwell (second-in-command), and captains Lloyd (Acting Adjutant), Macdonald, Whitehead, Kenworthy, and Aitken.

There were some 4,000 people packed into the square, and in this respect the spectacle achieved its aim as once the 'dismiss' was ordered, the recruiting meeting that followed was sure of a big success. The crowd was the biggest attracted to a Manchester recruiting meeting before or since that at Belle Vue. An address was then given by J. B. Martindale, the prospective Liberal candidate for Widnes and the organizing secretary of the Red Cross, East Lancashire Division. He reminded

Band practice on the patriotically adorned outdoor stage at Heaton Park Camp, April 1915.

the meeting of the great and glorious history of the Manchester Regiment and of its achievements in France so far. It was a speech designed to rouse the patriotic fervour of a partisan crowd and, as such, it was 'manufactured' to appeal to sentiment and recruitment figures. 'The battalions at Heaton Park have laboured in the vineyards for some months. They now ask you to join them at the eleventh hour at the same pay ... It is a glorious opportunity. Support the officers and men who are doing so much for you. Join the 17th Battalion, and make it complete.' (*MEN*, Tuesday, 16 February 1915 p. 5) Whilst this recruitment appeal was in progress men of the 17th Battalion worked their way through the crowd, repeating the same message to any likely looking candidates and onlookers.

By April 1915 the *Manchester Evening News* reported on further efforts by the City's battalions to boost recruiting. The report tells us that 159 enlistments had been obtained for various regiments, as well as sixty-one men taken on at Houldsworth Hall for the motor transport services. The South Lancashires had been recruiting successfully, as had the four City battalions at Heaton Park. The other four City battalions at Morecambe were still short of a full complement by around fifty men. At this time the City battalions at Heaton Park were about to depart for Grantham, where they would undergo further training, boosted by their enlistment of more 'citizen soldiers'.

The Manchester Regiment practising with Mills bombs at Heaton Park in 1915.

The City Pals battalions were first suggested at the end of August 1914, immediately after Lord Kitchener's first great appeal to the nation to raise an army of a million men. Young men from the Manchester business houses and home trades provided the necessary impetus at the start of the campaign, which rapidly developed into a great recruitment drive. Many inducements were offered to potential recruits by companies, such as a promise of half-wages whilst on service, and keeping their jobs open until their return. In addition a fund was raised for equipping the First Battalion. The drive was so successful that it was found four battalions could easily be raised, and the inducements and the equipment fund grew accordingly. Four battalions totalling a full brigade of around 5,000 men were raised in less than three weeks. Manchester town hall was made the chief recruiting station, and so enthusiastic was the rush to recruit in the initial stages of the drive that a further two battalions could easily have been raised in the first month. In fact, so prolific were Manchester's records of recruitment that special thanks for them were given in Parliament. Eventually, permission was given to raise the two further Pals battalions and a second brigade. Heaton Park, the White City and Belle Vue were all extensively utilized for training purposes.

Heaton Park was initially a tented training camp, but the onset of winter meant that more comfortable quarters were needed. These were provided by the erection of huts for the four battalions first raised – the 16th, 17th 18th and 19th service battalions of the Manchester Regiment. Meanwhile, whilst the second brigade was filling up, ideal training quarters were secured at Morecambe, and the 20th, 21st and 22nd battalions were moved there in complete strength at the end of the year. In order to complete the second brigade a Bantams' Battalion for 'smaller men' was formed; enlisting at Manchester town hall, they were immediately drafted off to Morecambe.

A memorial service at Manchester Cathedral in 1918 revealed another source of recruits. Canon Green spoke a few words in memory of the men who had fallen, who were members of the University and Public Schools Battalion. He emphasized the fact that few of those who joined the 30th Royal Fusiliers had ever given any consideration to a military life or matters pertaining to it. Their actions and sacrifice refuted the commonly held belief that young men of that time were not committed to any cause. Members of the Manchester Grammar School Officer Training Corps brought wreaths, which were afterwards laid on the monument to the Lancashire Fusiliers in St. Ann's Square, by the Lady Mayoress and her daughters. Today there are memorials at Manchester Grammar School and Manchester Cathedral. The *Manchester Evening News* summed up the scale of the grief and loss of the times by stating, 'Probably there were few in the large congregation who had not lost some relative at the historic Battle of the Somme, in which so large a number of Manchester's young manhood laid down their lives.'

Manchester's Great War Legacy at Sea

Manchester's position as a great inland port at the head of the Manchester Ship Canal was enhanced by Manchester Liners, whose seagoing vessels were purpose-built to navigate the canal, thus continuing the city's wartime effort. In August 1914 Manchester Liners had a fleet of fifteen ships which continued to operate services to ports in eastern Canada and the United States, returning with war and other supplies. *Manchester Miller* (1903) and *Manchester Civilian* (1913) were requisitioned as supply ships and sent with coal to the Falkland Islands to refuel the battlecruisers HMS *Inflexible* and HMS *Invincible*. As *Manchester Civilian* was coaling the cruisers, German vessels approached, causing the British warships to immediately cast off in order to engage the enemy. Admiral von Spee's battleships *Scharnhost* and *Gneisenau* and escorting cruisers were sunk. The *Manchester Civilian* was later fitted with minesweeper equipment and returned to the United Kingdom in 1916, carrying supplies and equipment from Canada to the troops in France. All Manchester Liners' vessels were fitted with defensive guns at the bow and stern. In June 1917 *Manchester Port* (1904) repelled a submarine attack with gunfire, near Cape Wrath. *Manchester Commerce* (1899), outward bound for Quebec City, was sunk off north-west Ireland on 26 October 1914, with the loss of fourteen crew members, becoming the first merchant ship to be sunk by a mine. The *Manchester Evening News* in March 1916 reports on the dramatic sinking of *Manchester Engineer*, in which *Manchester Commerce* is referred to, thus:

> The crew of the torpedoed steamer, Manchester Engineer, were landed at Queenstown last night, having been picked up by steamers from the sinking vessel. They numbered 33.

They said their steamer was struck yesterday morning at 7 o'clock by a German submarine. Friendly steamers were soon steaming to their assistance. That frightened the submarine, and she took her departure. The vessel, which was commanded by Captain J. Smith, and carried a crew of 35 to 40, is the second Manchester Liner lost in the war, the other being the Manchester Commerce, which went down not long after hostilities began somewhere to the North of Ireland.

The Manchester Engineer was one of the fine fleet of Manchester Liners trading between this country and America and Canada. She was a steel screw steamer of 4,302 tons gross, and was built by the Northumberland Shipbuilding Company Limited, at Newcastle, in 1902.

On 5 June 1917 the second *Manchester Trader*, en route from Souda Bay in Crete to Algiers, was involved in a running battle with U-66 before she was captured and sunk near Pantellaria Island, with the loss of one crew member. Captain F. D. Struss was awarded the Distinguished Service Cross and went on to serve with Manchester Liners for forty years. A further nine ships were sunk by U-boats, seven of the losses occurring in 1917. Between 1916 and 1918 Manchester Liners acquired seven ships, four of which were sunk in 1917. On 18 June 1917 the second *Manchester Engineer* (which had been acquired second-hand that year) was bound for Archangel and was chased by a U-boat. She escaped, however, when her naval escort arrived. On 16 August 1917, when sailing from the Tyne to St Nazaire with coal, she was torpedoed 5 miles off Flamborough Head and sunk. *Manchester Division* was on her maiden voyage from West Hartlepool to join a westbound Atlantic convoy at Plymouth when she rammed and sank a German submarine off Flamborough Head in October 1918. At the end of the war, in November 1918, Manchester Liners had twelve surviving vessels on its books.

Manchester Liners had served the city and country well in the Great War, with its legacy of providing goods, raw materials and war supplies for the war effort, a legacy which was to continue into World War Two. The Manchester Regiment had also made many sacrifices in terms of men and resources, and in 1922 the city and regiment were honoured when Manchester Liners took delivery of the *Manchester Regiment*. The original *Manchester Regiment* sank in 1939 and was replaced by a new vessel, built c. 1950.

The *Manchester Evening News* tells us of a U-boat assault on the steamer *Aguila*, which was torpedoed off the Pembrokeshire coast on 27 March 1915. This story gives us an indication of the perilous existence merchant vessels endured when they took to sea during times of U-boat activity. The story was told by J. J. M'Mahon, of Queens Road, Manchester, who was an electrical engineer in the Overhead Department of Manchester Corporation, and who injured his shoulder and burned his hand during escape in a lifeboat. Mr M'Mahon had been in ill health and was bound for the Canary Islands on the *Aguila* when the steamer was torpedoed. The passengers had spotted a German submarine, which was U-28, coming alongside. The *Aguila*'s captain tried to elude the submarine by altering the vessel's course, which alerted the German commander, who then started to shell the vessel, aiming at the bows and the wireless equipment, which he struck.

MANCHESTER LINERS LTD.   S.S. "MANCHESTER REGIMENT"   Gross Tonnage 7638

SS *Manchester Regiment* c. 1950.

The *Manchester Regiment* had a crew of sixty-five and was the largest Manchester Liners' vessel operated to date, carrying 512 cattle plus hold cargo, and was equipped with large derricks in order to assist manoeuvring heavy goods. The vessel's record from the Mersey Bar to Quebec was seven days and nine hours. In 1929 *Manchester Regiment* steamed 160 miles through a gale in order to reach the sinking Glasgow steamer *Volumnia*. A lifeboat was launched, rescuing the crew of forty-five. King George V awarded the lifeboat's crew the Silver Medal for Gallantry in Saving Life at Sea, and Manchester's Lord Mayor presented a silver salver from the Board of Trade to Captain Linton. On the night of 4 December 1939 *Manchester Regiment's* captain, E. W. Raper, and a crew of seventy-four, were in convoy 150 miles south-west of Cape Race. A vessel had just been sunk and the SS *Oropesa* was returning to the convoy with forty-two survivors when she collided with the *Manchester Regiment*. She did not sink at once, giving Captain Raper time to transfer fifty of his crew to the *Oropesa* and continue trying to save her. Captain Raper lowered a lifeboat, manned by seventeen men, including himself, as he wished to confer with his opposite number on the *Oropesa*. However, the boat capsized, drowning seven men and effectively ending any attempts to save the *Manchester Regiment*, which sank soon afterwards. Nine people died in the collision. (www.wrecksite.eu)

Originally built in 1905 as the *Craigvar* for the West of Scotland Steam Ship Co., in 1910 the Treasury Steam Ship Co bought her and renamed her *Nation*. In 1917 Manchester Liners bought her and renamed her *Manchester Engineer*, replacing a previous ship of the same name sunk by a U-boat in 1916. In August 1917 UC-16 torpedoed and sank the second *Manchester Engineer* southeast of Flamborough Head in Yorkshire.

According to the narrator the U-boat commander gave them very little time to make for the lifeboats. Several passengers got into one and cast off into a heavy sea, taking care to keep clear of the ship and potential impact. Whilst they were doing this they witnessed Chief Engineer Edwards falling into the sea, with the general opinion being that he had been shot by the Germans. Meanwhile, the other lifeboat capsized and its occupants were thrown into the sea. Three people were picked up but a fourth, a woman, disappeared from view before she could be reached. All this was overlooked by the U-boat, which remained a few hundred feet away. According to Mr M'Mahon, 'Most of the crew were standing on the deck with folded arms laughing at our misfortune. They made no attempt to save us: they appeared to gloat over the terrible scene.' The lifeboat departed, with the *Aguila* on fire amidships, sinking by the stern and breaking in two. Some of the crew sang in order to keep spirits up, but were deterred by gunfire from the U-boat.

Eventually, at about 4.30 a.m., some twelve hours after manning the lifeboats, they were picked up by the *Lady Plymouth*, a collier bound for Buenos Aires. They estimated that the waves were averaging a height of 32–35 feet and that they had drifted about 36 miles in the direction of Queenstown. At Madeira the *Lady Plymouth* was met by a British cruiser and escorted into the bay. M'Mahon returned on the *Walmer Castle* from Cape Town, and in conclusion he stated, 'They are not pirates, they are outlaws. They did not give us any time to get away; they simply peppered us with shot. Three or four of the crew were killed and several were wounded.'

Zeppelin Raids

We tend to think of air raids as being a phenomenon associated with the Second World War, and the Blitz of 1940; but whilst air flight was still in its infancy, each side had its squadrons of fighters and bombers, although their range was somewhat limited. However, there were no such restrictions for the German's Zeppelin airships, which posed a threat to the capital and the east coast of England throughout the war. In one case, as reported by the *Manchester Evening News* in October 1917, they were allegedly active across the whole country. Unfortunately, from the German point of view, the Zeppelins were at the mercy of any sudden change in weather conditions, or a dramatic shift of the wind direction or speed. They remained cumbersome and could not cope with the speed and agility of the technologically advancing aeroplane. For their crews conditions remained very primitive and they needed to be physically strong to survive a long mission at altitude and in freezing conditions. The *Manchester Evening News* reports on the capture of a Zeppelin crew involved in the raids, which included Manchester, telling us that,

Zeppelin airship c. 1930, showing the scale involved in airship production, design and flight.

The nineteen men composing the crew immediately jumped to earth. The last of these was the commander, who arranged his men in good order and gave them their final instructions and then discharged his pistol into the envelope of the balloon. Realising that he intended to set it on fire, and determined to prevent this at all costs I, who was standing thirty yards away, loaded my sporting rifle and shouted 'stop or I fire'. The threat was sufficient, and the commander threw down his pistol and held up his arms, crying 'Kamerad'. Then the Germans stood quiet, while I continued to watch them, ready to fire on the first who should attempt to flee. Soon a crowd gathered round the airship, and we were able to place the crew under a strong guard. The commander seemed to be furious, but the men appeared delighted. They were stalwart fellows, warmly clothed in leather combinations, and had evidently been chosen for their powers of physical endurance ... It appears that she was one of the squadron returning from the raid in England, which was diverted from its proper course by contrary winds.

According to Berlin, on the night of Friday 19 October / Saturday 20 October 1917 a naval airship squadron under Captain Baron Prensch von Buttlen Braudeniels attacked towns and cities across a broad swathe of England, including London, Manchester, Birmingham, Nottingham, Derby, Lowestoft, Hull, Grimsby, Norwich, and Mappleton. On the return journey, owing to adverse winds and deteriorating weather conditions including dense mist, four airships, commanded by captains Herbert, Koolle, Hans Geyer, and Schnander, drifted over the Western Front. According to French official communications, they were

On 19 January 1915 German Zeppelins launched the first air attacks over England. Invented by Count von Zeppelin, a retired German Army officer, the Zeppelin was lighter than air, being filled with hydrogen and constructed of fabric over a steel framework. In 1914 Germany had several Zeppelins, each capable of a speed approaching 85mph and carrying up to 2 tons of bombs. By 1915, with a stalemate along the Western Front, the Germans decided to use their new airborne weapon against Britain. The first raid took place against the eastern coastal towns of Great Yarmouth and King's Lynn on 19 January 1915. Britain's first ever air-raid casualties were seventy-two-year-old Martha Taylor and shoemaker Samuel Smith. By using the Zeppelins on civilian targets the Germans hoped to break civilian morale and force the British government to give up their pursuit of a European war. Bombing also took place against many other towns in eastern and south-eastern England, including Southend, Ipswich and Bury St Edmunds. London was hit several times, with Stoke Newington the first London target of an air raid. The propaganda value of these raids was immense, for both sides. Eventually the Zeppelin's weak point was discovered and exploited by explosive bullets that set the hydrogen alight.

either shot down or forced down. The Zeppelins responsible for the raids over England met with disaster on their return journeys. Four were brought down by French anti-aircraft fire or by Allied airmen. A fifth was destroyed, with three more still airborne over France or the Mediterranean at the time of the report.

The night of 19/20 October 1917 was the last major Zeppelin raid of the war, with thirteen airships heading for the north of England's major industrial centres of Sheffield, Manchester and Liverpool. All the Zeppelins were debilitated by an unexpected and exceptionally strong headwind at altitude, as reported at the time; for example, L45 attempted to reach Sheffield but instead was forced to drop its bombs on Northampton and London, giving an indication of how far off course the headwinds were pushing the Zeppelins. L45 reduced altitude to try and escape the winds, but was forced back to the higher air by defensive aeroplane activity. The Zeppelin then had engine failure in three engines and was blown over France, landing near Sisteron, where the crew set it on fire and surrendered. As reported in the *Manchester Evening News*, the other Zeppelins involved in the raid fared no better, succumbing to a combination of ground and airborne fire, engine failure, the weather and impact damage. There were no more raids in 1917, but they did continue in 1918, after the Zeppelins had been fitted with new, more powerful engines. Whilst air flight was still in its infancy at the conclusion of the First World War, the legacy of the raids reported in Manchester's press was to have deadly, long-term consequences by the time of the outbreak of the Second World War in 1939.

Peace celebrations at Station Road Bridge, Urmston.

5. THE HOME FRONT, AIR RAIDS AND THE LEGACY OF THE MANCHESTER REGIMENT IN THE SECOND WORLD WAR

Manchester and the Christmas Blitz of 1940

The Christmas Blitz, on the nights of 22/23 and 23/24 December 1940, killed hundreds of people and caused widespread destruction to the infrastructure of city centre Manchester. Shops and buildings in the St Ann's district were reduced to ruins and the area around Deansgate, close to Manchester Cathedral, was severely affected. A large bomb crater showed onlookers where the point of impact had been. Buildings burned throughout the night and into the following day and masonry from bombed-out buildings came crashing down, perilously close to the fire services and ambulance rescue crews. Thick smoke and dust reduced visibility and hampered any rescue efforts. On the first night two waves of German bombing hit the city, starting

The Royal Exchange, junction of Cross Street and Market Street, in 1910, survivor of the Manchester Blitz of 1940.

The Shambles, Manchester   Valentines Series

The Old Wellington Inn, Shambles Square, Market Place, in 1903, survivor of the Manchester Blitz of 1940.

at 2000 hours on 22 December and continuing until 0600 hours on 23 December. Among the buildings hit in the city centre were the Free Trade Hall on Peter Street, Cross Street Chapel, the Royal Exchange, Smithfield Market, Chetham's Hospital, the Gaiety Theatre, the medieval heart of the old market town at Shambles Square (only the Wellington Inn and Sinclairs survive today), and St Ann's Church in St Ann's Square. Only one English cathedral, at Coventry, took more bombardment than Manchester Cathedral.

In total 684 people died and a further 2,300 were wounded, with districts to the north and east of the city badly affected, notably Cheetham Hill and Strangeways. At least 8,000 homes were made uninhabitable. Bombing campaigns on two consecutive nights was a tactic used by the Luftwaffe in order to inflict maximum disruption and destruction on its intended targets. On the first night 272 tons of high-explosive bombs were dropped by 270 aircraft. The following night another 195 tons of high explosives were dropped on the city by 171 aircraft. Over the course of two nights, almost 2,000 incendiary bombs were also dropped on Manchester. One side of Piccadilly was almost completely destroyed in the raids. Around 600 fires were started by incendiary bombs over the two nights, decimating warehouse and commercial premises.

Between 1939 and 1945, 1,400 civilians died in Manchester, so the Christmas Blitz represents nearly half of the total deaths. One in ten of these victims were under the

Parker Street, Piccadilly, and repair of blitz damage.

age of thirteen. Those whose homes became uninhabitable would break up furniture in their gardens in order to build fires for cooking. Broken water mains led to contamination and meant that drinking water had to be provided from bowsers. Electricity was rationed, and broken gas mains also led to further hazards, especially if accompanied by incendiary bombs and the 'firestorm' phenomenon. Of course, the Luftwaffe's bombing was not always as accurate as intended and sometimes a bomb-load would be jettisoned in haste to avoid anti-aircraft fire, so suburbs immediately surrounding the city centre were also bombed. These included Ancoats, home to many mills and factories, including an important Avro aircraft factory, making parts for Lancaster and Manchester bombers. Salford and Stretford were also badly affected. Around 215 people were killed and 910 injured in Salford. In Stretford seventy-three were killed, and the following month there was a prolonged air raid which hit Old Trafford and lasted for three hours. Air raids continued and on Christmas Eve 1944 Heinkel 111 bombers flying over the Yorkshire coast launched forty-five flying bombs at Manchester. A V1 landed in the city centre, while twenty-seven people in neighbouring Oldham were killed by a stray bomb. Another seventeen were killed elsewhere and 109 wounded. Fortunately, Manchester was beyond the range of V2 rockets.

The Luftwaffe's objective of the bombing campaign across Britain was to disrupt the country's industrial base by targeting ports and centres of distribution. Coventry had been bombed in the previous month because it was a centre of heavy industry. British intelligence rightly anticipated that there would be further bombing

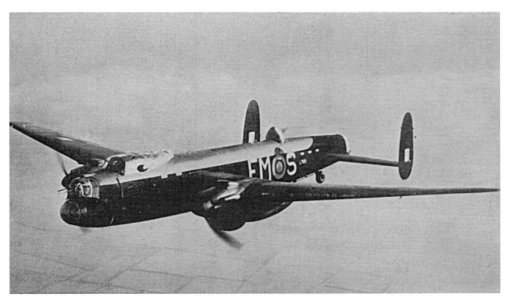

Forerunner to the massively successful Lancaster heavy bomber, the Avro Manchester medium bomber saw only limited service. Both aircraft were produced at Avro's Trafford Park works.

The V1 (Vengeance Weapon) was developed at Peenemunde Army Research Centre on the Baltic coast, by the Luftwaffe. Designed by Fritz Gosslau for the terror bombing of London, the first V1s were fired from the French and Dutch coasts due to limited range. Their use peaked in 1944–45. The V1 was capable of killing many, injuring large numbers and causing a great deal of structural damage and destruction to buildings over a wide area. The initial explosion of a V1 led to the creation of a vacuum, which produced a pushing and pulling effect on surrounding buildings, leading to total destruction. The blast area extended from 400 to 600 yards in each direction. Approximately 6,184 people were killed by the V1 and 17,981 seriously injured. The V2 (Retribution Weapon) was the world's first, long-range, guided, ballistic missile, fuelled by a liquid-propellant rocket engine. The V2 became the first artificial object to cross the boundary of space, on 20 June 1944. It was developed by Wernher von Braun. The V2 weighed 13 tons, produced a sonic boom from the upper atmosphere, and reached speeds of 3,000mph or 4,828kph on impact. It had been known about by British intelligence for some time, but it was assumed the launch sites were overrun during the Allied invasion of Normandy. An estimated 9,000 civilians died as a result of V2 attacks.

"THE PROFICIENCY TEST" SERIES   No.—5

THE AVRO MANCHESTER I.

BRITISH HEAVY BOMBER.

2 Rolls Royce Vulture 24 cylinder X type aero motors neatly cowled into wing with radiators below. 3 blade D.H. Hydromatic constant-speed air screws. Mid-wing monoplane. Heavily armed with a two-gun turret in the nose, two-gun turret on top of fuselage and a Nash and Thompson 4-gun turret in tail. All metal stressed skin construction. Crew of 7.

Dimensions.—Span, 90 ft. 1 in.; length, 70 ft.; height, 19 ft. 6 in. No other data available for publication.

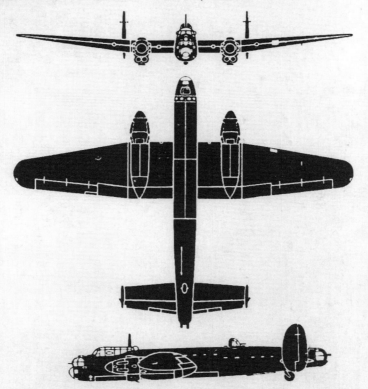

THESE DRAWINGS, REPRODUCED FROM "AIRCRAFT IDENTIFICATION," ARE THE COPYRIGHT OF "THE AEROPLANE."

RECOGNITION POINTS.—Two motor mid-wing monoplane. Rectangular centre section. Outer wings swept back at leading edge. Some versions have single central fin and twin fins and rudders, others tall twin fins and rudders. Deep almost untapered fuselage with slight slope of top line towards tail turret. Tail wheel does not retract.

Avro Manchester heavy bomber recognition card, for use by air raid precaution wardens during air raids and air watch duties.

campaigns, but could not foresee their intensity and ferocity. Manchester was home to the major industrial centre of Trafford Park, the largest industrial estate in Europe, and was seen as an extension to the port of Liverpool, with its own port and canal link. Therefore, it was an obvious target. Trafford Park was home to the Avro aircraft manufacturer, which produced Manchester and Lancaster bombers. Ford also employed 17,000 workers making aircraft engines at Trafford Park. During the raids, the Metropolitan Vickers complex on Westinghouse Road was badly damaged, and in a later raid of 11 March 1941 aimed at the Trafford Park industrial estate, Manchester United Football Club's ground at Old Trafford was hit by a bomb, destroying the pitch and demolishing the stands. It was rebuilt after the war and reopened in 1949. Until then the club had to play all their home fixtures at neighbouring Maine Road, the home of Manchester City Football Club.

Manchester's first air raid was in September 1940, when the Palace Theatre on Oxford Street was bombed. There was another major raid on 2 June 1941, when the worst of the blitz was thought to be over. This saw the old Salford Royal Hospital on Chapel Street bombed, with fourteen nurses killed. The same raid damaged the police headquarters. From September 1940 to May 1941, the main period of the blitz, there were three major raids (100 tons or more of high-explosive bombs dropped on an identified target). Overall, around 578 tons of high-explosive bombs fell on Manchester, making it the eleventh most heavily raided area of Britain; neighbouring Liverpool and Birkenhead were the second most blitzed areas. The *Manchester Guardian* reported on the first night of bombing, 23 December 1940, telling us that

Westinghouse works, Westinghouse Road, Trafford Park, in 1908. Shown is one of the production sheds and the heavy electrical engineering the plant specialized in. It was later utilized in the production of heavy bombers, which is the reason why it became the target of numerous bombing campaigns.

Bomb damage at Old Trafford football ground, home of Manchester United Football Club. Structural damage was not fully repaired until 1949. The ground's proximity to Trafford Park industrial estate led to its destruction.

Air-raid damage in Manchester. The fire services worked frantically to limit the damage, often amid falling masonry and bombs.

hundreds of incendiary bombs and many high explosives were dropped, leading to numerous fires in different areas of the city. Firemen worked throughout the barrage and amid falling bombs.

The attack lasted 'many hours' and began just after darkness had fallen, whilst many people were returning from their work and were caught in the streets. Anti-aircraft fire was deployed against the Luftwaffe's bombers, but it was Manchester's worst experience of bombing. A number of people were trapped in a public air-raid shelter beneath a building that was hit by a high-explosive bomb. The vast majority were rescued but it took several hours of digging through the rubble, much of it by hand. 'One of the first high-explosive bombs to fall on the city trapped 450 people in a shelter below a building which was so damaged that it was expected to fall in at any moment. It was impossible to say what had happened, but many hours later the dogged work of the rescuers having gone on in spite of fires and bombs and falling stones, it was believed that everyone had been got out. Sometime after this bomb fell it was reported that a number of people were trapped in a hotel, and other buildings in the city were set on fire.'

Shops, business premises, public buildings and hospitals were among the places hit. Three schools were damaged by fire caused by incendiary bombs. Dozens of incendiary bombs fell in the streets, with passers-by using sandbags to smother the flames. The sandbags had been placed at convenient places such as street corners for use in such an emergency. Several incendiaries fell in Piccadilly Gardens, and buses that had been pulled up there in order to allow people to take cover were set on fire. Manchester's newspaper offices were also hit by incendiary bombs, but the office firefighters put out the flames before any damage was done. Fire-watchers were commonly used throughout the war and were useful for both putting out incendiary fires, spotting fires on neighbouring buildings, and alerting the relevant A.R.P. (Air Raid Precautions) authorities.

'In another part of the town' incendiary bombs fell into the grounds of a hospital (Manchester Royal Infirmary), and 'one or two penetrated the roofs of empty wards. Nurses assisted the fire squads in dealing with them and no serious damage was reported'. Two patients and a nurse were slightly injured when the wing of another hospital was damaged. Nobody else in the building was hurt. A third hospital was also hit. The Luftwaffe used the tactic of scattering incendiaries about their target, followed by high explosives, which caused damage to houses and led to many injuries. 'In an outlying district a public house was hit and a number of people were trapped in the wreckage. Rescue squads worked strenuously to release them.' At Clopton Street, Hulme, one of the worst incidents of the Christmas Blitz occurred when a bomb struck the Manley Arms public house. The occupants, who were celebrating at a wedding party, lost more than a dozen of their number in this one attack.

At the time of the Manchester Blitz, many of the city's full- and part-time firefighters and Civil Defence workers were still in Liverpool, where they had been sent several days before to combat fires caused by raids there – hence, Manchester's devastation was compounded by this decision. However, on the 24 December 1940 the *Manchester*

After the First World War it was predicted that in any future war there would be large-scale bombing of the British civilian population, leading to huge casualties. In April 1937, in response to this fear, an Air Raid Warden's service was created. By 1939 there were around 1.5 million in the Air Raid Precautions, or Civil Defence. Air Raid Wardens were its best-known creation and were local, needing to know a district and its people. Their main duties were to register everyone in their sector and enforce the blackout. They helped people to the nearest shelters during air raids and then toured their sector, usually in pairs, at great personal risk. They would also regularly check those in the air-raid shelter, deal with casualties, put out fires and organize emergency services. Most were part-time volunteers with full-time jobs. In May 1941 full-time and regular part-time wardens were issued with blue serge uniforms. Every local council was responsible for organizing Air Raid Precaution Wardens, messengers, ambulance drivers, rescue parties and liaison with police and fire brigades. During the war almost 7,000 Civil Defence workers were killed. A total of 1.4 million people served as Air Raid Precaution Wardens during the Second World War, before the service was stood down on 2 May 1945.

Manchester Royal Infirmary, Oxford Road, in 1908. In the blitz of December 1940 extensive damage was caused to the hospital.

Guardian tells us that, 'An attack on a North-western town on Sunday night brought out the finest qualities of the A.R.P. workers, whose untiring efforts undoubtedly lessened the extent of the damage.' Manchester's transport infrastructure was destroyed, with its main train stations damaged, and main road routes of Deansgate and Oxford Road into the city blocked by fallen debris from bombed-out buildings, bomb craters, mines and unexploded bombs. As a result, part of the city centre had to be cordoned off. The *Manchester Guardian* of 24 December 1940 describes wrecked buildings and a church with only its four walls left standing. A high-explosive bomb wrecked a block at a hospital, causing the deaths of the medical superintendent, his wife, the matron, and the wife of the hospital steward. Both the doctor and the matron had served the hospital for many years. However, due to censorship restrictions, the *Manchester Guardian* does not name the hospital involved. On the first night of the raid bombs struck the Manchester Royal Infirmary, and most of the windows were blown out. A total of 10,000 panes of glass had to be replaced. On the second night, 23/24 December 1940, a delayed-action-fuse bomb fell on the X-ray and teaching block and damaged the tower. The bomb subsequently exploded on the following day, 24 December 1940, putting the heating of the entire hospital out of action and causing the tower to collapse. There were no casualties to patients or staff, but extensive demolition was subsequently required to the affected hospital buildings. This was not the first time that the hospital had been affected by bombing. On 11 October 1940 the nurses' home took a direct hit from a high-explosive bomb. In the basement shelters were 112 nurses, but nobody was hurt.

The *Manchester Guardian* further tells us that many schools were damaged by indirect hits and blasts. Many were also made homeless as a result of the bombing. In order to provide for them the emergency housing and feeding scheme of the Public Assistance authorities was utilized. Those who called at the offices could rest in the waiting room and were then taken by special buses to emergency rest centres, including a number of schools, whose cooking facilities were made available to them, until permanent accommodation was provided. Many of those who presented themselves had only the clothes they stood up in and, 'although the number of casualties is not known it is feared that the total of killed and injured may be heavy as a result of the damage in densely populated areas'. The official report tells us that, 'Enemy activity on Sunday night was mainly directed against a city [Manchester] in the North-West, which was heavily attacked for many hours. A large number of fires were caused, and considerable damage was done to buildings and shops in the city. Fuller reports as to the casualties are not yet available, but it is known that a number of people were killed and many others injured. Bombs were also dropped on Merseyside and in the East Midlands. In these areas little damage was done and casualties were slight. In the South of England some houses were damaged and a small number of people were killed and others injured. Two enemy bombers were destroyed.'

An official German war report in the *Manchester Guardian* (24 December 1940) tells us that, 'During last night large formations of our heavy bombers attacked with great success the important industrial centre of Manchester. Huge fires were caused in factories and warehouses.' And a further headline in the *Manchester Guardian* states, 'NIGHT RAIDERS AGAIN IN THE NORTH-WEST. Raids again started soon after darkness fell, with incendiary and high-explosive bombs falling on the city. The attack was concentrated in one area of the city, where fires had been started. Commercial buildings were again heavily damaged and set alight despite some fierce anti-aircraft fire. A chapel [Cross Street] was hit by incendiaries and set alight. High explosives caused extensive damage to dwelling houses, public buildings, cinemas and hospitals. There were many casualties and some deaths. One hospital was severely damaged [Manchester Royal Infirmary], but there were no reports of any casualties. One enemy raider was shot down at Old Trafford.'

A further official statement in the *Manchester Guardian* (24 December 1940) tells us, 'Manchester took the full force of Sunday night's Nazi attack on the civilians of Britain.' Shortly after dark the white light of flares lit up the city and incendiary bombs were dropped. Wave upon wave of bombers swept over the burning buildings of Manchester and dropped high-explosive bombs among the men already working to smother the flames. However, according to the town clerk, R. H. Adcock, many hours of intense bombing had produced a surprisingly small number of casualties. The main problem was that of homelessness caused by severe bomb damage.

There were other hazards too, unforeseen before the bombing campaign on the city. People spectating were hampering the work of the Civil Defence Services. The *Manchester Guardian* requested that they refrain from this activity and also issued a warning in relation to fire-watching, which tells us, 'The Ministry of Information announced that the people responsible in certain buildings had apparently neglected their legal obligation to provide an efficient service of fire-watchers. It warns that this obligation will be enforced most vigorously by prosecution. The raid began with a lavish distribution of incendiary bombs – a great many of which were disposed of by fire-watchers, and in some cases even by people in the street. But it soon became apparent that buildings had ignited in several directions. There was some excitement as fire-watchers functioning on some of the city's buildings endeavoured to call attention to incendiary bombs that were apparently burning unhindered.'

Many were made homeless by the bombing and a number of people were unable to remain in their homes as the result of the suspected presence of unexploded bombs. The *Manchester Guardian* gives us the names of some of the victims of the bombing and the circumstances surrounding their involvement, and reminds us of the real tragedy behind these stories. 'Mr. and Mrs. D. Paton, who had until shortly before the raid always sheltered with neighbours, were killed outright in their house. Three other people are buried and believed to be dead in another house which had no shelter. One body has been recovered. Mr H. E. Hanson, whose house was destroyed, was sheltering with his family and they all escaped, although the shock threw them into a heap at the end of the shelter.' The Auxiliary Fire Service was quick to deal with the outbreak of fires. One of the first men killed was in the Auxiliary Fire Service, and another early casualty was a policeman. The bravery of those involved in the rescue operations was emphasized.

'The same diffidence has been shown here by the men of the civilian defence services as has been evident in other places – each is most ready to talk about the achievements of the others. A fireman, black and grimy, tired and hungry, after hours of incessant work, was full of praise for a policeman who had helped him to burrow under a damaged house in which a woman was trapped. A policeman did homage in broken sentences to the A.F.S. while railing good-naturedly at people who would walk under the walls of buildings in danger of collapsing. One group of firemen could talk of nothing but the courage of three girls who stayed in town all night making cups of tea and carrying them round to the pump teams. "Nothing would stop them," one of these men told me. "I am sure any one of us would die for them; they walked about as calmly as if they were serving afternoon tea in their own houses. And a cup of tea is a grand thing when life is hot and dusty and dangerous!"'

The Manchester Regiment in the Second World War

Whilst the people of Manchester were enduring their own battles on the Home Front, the Manchester Regiment were taking the fight to the Germans across north-west Europe and Italy. In May 1940 Germany invaded France. The 2nd, 5th, and 9th battalions formed part of the British Expeditionary Force – the 2nd and 9th were machine-gun battalions. The British Expeditionary Force was eventually pushed back to Dunkirk, where 330,000 were evacuated. Of the surviving men of the 2nd Manchesters, more than 300 were evacuated, with around 200 remaining to engage the Germans in a rearguard action, until they were

Vickers machine guns of 1/7th Manchester Regiment set up outside shops in St Pol, France, 8 March 1940. Note the French troops in their greatcoats. (Photo Lt L. A. Puttnam / War Office via IWM)

captured or killed. The 5th and 9th battalions were also evacuated, having suffered light casualties, with evacuation ending on 3 June 1940.

In the summer of 1944, the battalion acted as the Royal Bodyguard at Balmoral Castle while the Royal Family was in residence and then served as a machine-gun battalion with the 55th (West Lancs) Infantry Division until the end of the war. On 27 June 1944 the 1st Battalion Manchester Regiment landed in France, twenty-one days after the D-Day landings on 6 June 1944. With the rest of the 53rd Division, the battalion experienced some fierce fighting in the Battle of Normandy. It took part in engagements around Caen, which was captured by British and Canadian forces on 9 July 1944. The *Manchester Evening News* tells us of the D-Day invasion, when 'naval forces, supported by strong air forces, began landing Allied armies on the northern coast of France'. A beachhead was secured by British and Canadian troops at Normandy and the Allies were 'slashing their way ahead'. Allied forces also landed at Arromanches, a fishing port 15 miles north-west of Caen, with parachutists reported in the Channel Isles of Jersey and Guernsey. They were at once engaged by the Germans. The troops from Arromanches had penetrated several miles to the south-east of Caen and Isigny and Paris Radio said 'The enemy is retreating deeper inland.' Whilst these battles developed, the 1st, 2nd and 6th British airborne divisions were engaged in the Seine Estuary.

Further reports said that eighty Allied warships were approaching Cherbourg and other landing craft were heading from England. Allied forces began their umbrella bombardment as soon as dawn broke. 'It seemed that hell itself had been let loose. From left, right and centre our guns opened up and from our vantage point at sea we could see that targets ashore were being pounded out of existence as the assaulting infantry sailed slowly and surely ahead to let bayonets do whatever work remained. From sea and sky the bombardment continued until our infantry went ashore. It was a magnificent sight. Wave upon wave of khaki-clad figures surged up the beaches overcoming any opposition in their way, and surging on.' In the House of Commons statements were made, 'I would like to express my own feelings and, I think, the feelings of every Member of this House, that our hearts and our thoughts are with those lads and the mothers who are at home.' There was a 'murmur of sympathetic cheering' after this comment; Churchill and Lloyd George then shook hands on announcement of the landings.

In July and August the 1st Battalion Manchester Regiment advanced across Northern France, reaching Antwerp, in Belgium, in early September. The 1st Manchesters and the rest of the 53rd (Welsh) Division moved to Turnhout before later advancing into the Netherlands, where the 1st and 7th Manchesters were involved in some fierce action. The 7th were now part of the 52nd (Lowland) Infantry Division and fought in the Battle of the Scheldt, under the command of the 1st Canadian Army. The 1st Manchesters entered Germany and crossed the Rhine with the 53rd Division in late March 1945. The 7th Manchesters, with the 52nd Division, saw its last engagement in Bremen, when the city was captured on 26 April 1945. The 1st Battalion ended the war in Hamburg, when the city surrendered on 3 May 1945.

The 8th (Ardwick) Battalion had been serving alongside the 5th Manchesters in the 127th Brigade of the 42nd Division until 5 May 1940, when the battalion was transferred to Malta. Both the 8th and 9th Manchesters took part in the Italian campaign. The 9th Manchesters were heavily involved in the fighting in August and September 1944. They served in Greece, during the civil war, and then returned to Italy until the end of the campaign there, and then reached Graz, Austria, by the end of the war. At home in Manchester 'Victory in Europe Day' celebrated an end to six years of conflict. At exactly 9.32 p.m. peace was declared and the people of Manchester thronged the streets to rejoice at the news. Street parties and 'singalongs' were organized and the city centre was soon filled with celebrating crowds, bunting and flags making it a festive occasion. Huge crowds gathered at Piccadilly Gardens and even more flocked to Albert Square, with the mayor addressing the crowds and Churchill making a radio address to the nation at 3.00 p.m. The *Manchester Evening News* reported on this and other celebrations from around the region on Tuesday 8 May 1945, telling us that Winston Churchill announced the official peace from midnight and that there were cheering crowds and crackers on the streets of Manchester. 'Several thousand joyous but not hysterical people gathered in Albert Square at 3 o'clock to hear the Prime Minister announce that the war in Europe, the greatest in history, was ended.' The crowds listened to the Police Band, waving and cheering, whilst fireworks exploded around the Square. After Churchill's speech, the cheering began again and the Union Jack was raised. There was a peal from the town hall bells, and the Lord Mayor, Alderman W. P. Jackson, spoke from the town hall steps. The flags of forty-four nations flew and the band played national anthems of the Allies. 'But the biggest cheer of all was reserved for what was hoped was the last all-clear.'

The Manchester Regiment also saw service in the Far East and was stationed in Singapore from 1938. The 1st Battalion Manchester Regiment, as part of the 2nd Malaya Infantry Brigade, saw action during the Japanese invasion of the island in February 1942. The surrender of Singapore was signed on 15 February 1942 by Lieutenant General Arthur Percival. Around 80,000 British and Commonwealth troops became prisoners of war of the Imperial Japanese Army. The 1st Battalion was reformed in the United Kingdom by the redesignation of the 6th Battalion.

In 1942, the 2nd Manchesters were sent to India with the rest of the British 2nd Infantry Division, being stationed first in British India, then Burma in 1944. The battalion was involved in the Battle of Kohima, in fierce fighting against the Japanese. It fought further actions in Burma until April 1945, when it returned to India. 'Victory in Japan Day' was declared on Wednesday 15 August 1945, with yet more celebrations at Albert Square. The *Manchester Evening News* gave some detail about these celebrations around the region. The end of the war was marked by two-day holidays in the United Kingdom, United States and Australia. At midnight Prime Minister Clement Atlee confirmed the news in a broadcast, which coincided with the *State Opening of Parliament*. Later, at 9.00 p.m., the King addressed the nation and the Empire in a broadcast from his study at Buckingham Palace. Crowds of people poured out onto the streets of every town and city, shouting, singing, dancing, lighting bonfires and letting off fireworks, in scenes very much like VE Day.

'In every town there was dancing in public squares, fireworks and bonfires, as well as bands and torchlight processions.' A Japanese flag captured by a Canadian Sergeant in the Far

Presentation to HRH Queen Elizabeth (Elizabeth Bowes-Lyon, later the Queen Mother) by the Manchester Regiment in 1948.

East fighting was publicly burned in Blackburn's Town Hall Square. Throughout the country flags of the Allied nations flew from public buildings. There were thanksgiving services in all churches, hymns were sung at cenotaphs, and there was much community singing. In many Lancashire towns transport was stopped and the cotton mills were closed. A crowd of around 10,000 paraded on Blackpool promenade and in Morecambe around 4,000 descended on Happy Mount Park, but 'there was very little boisterous celebrating as intoxicating liquor is in short supply. Owing to the non-arrival of beer several public houses cannot open today'.

After the war the 1st Manchesters remained in Germany as part of the British Army of the Rhine, until it returned to Britain in 1947, where it was joined by the 2nd Battalion. On 1 June 1948, the two battalions amalgamated in the presence of the regiment's Colonel-in-Chief, Queen Elizabeth (later the Queen Mother). Soon afterwards the 1st Battalion was posted to Germany. In 1951 the battalion was posted to Malaya, serving for three years in the Malayan emergency, where they had fifteen men killed in action. Then in 1958 the regiment was amalgamated with the King's Regiment (Liverpool) to create the King's Regiment. The monuments of Manchester commemorate those who gave their lives, protecting their city and country during two world wars. Their legacy is a city rebuilt from the ashes of that conflict, a city which remains vibrant and positive to this day. Manchester is their memorial.

BIBLIOGRAPHY

Chapter 1

Archaeology in Greater Manchester, *Castleshaw Roman Fort* (Greater Manchester Archaeological Unit, 1986)

Andrew, S., Bruton, F.A., Lees, W., *Excavation of the Roman Forts at Castleshaw (near Delph, West Riding) First and Second Interim Reports* (Manchester: University Press. 1908, 1911)

Arrowsmith, P., The Population of Manchester from c. AD79 to 1801 in *Journal of the Greater Manchester Archaeological Unit* (Vol. I. 1985 pp. 99-102)

Bruton, F.A., ed., *The Roman Fort at Manchester* (Manchester: University Press, 1909)

Flavius Vegetius Renatus. *Rei Militaris Instituta*. (Concerning Military Affairs)

Jackson in *Transactions of the Lancashire and Cheshire Antiquarian Society*. (Vol. XLIX. 1933 pp. 104-12)

Mamucium www.7agesofmanchester.org

Obituary, C. Roeder. *Manchester City News*, 16 September 1911.

Obituary, Dr. F.A. Bruton. *Manchester Guardian*, 15 January 1930 p. 14.

Obituary, Dr. F.A. Bruton. *Ulula,* January, 1930.

Roeder, C., *Roman Manchester* (Manchester: Gill. 1900 pp. 59-116)

Roman Manchester www.bbc.co.uk/manchester

Walker, J., Summary of the Development of Early Manchester in *Roman Manchester. A Frontier Settlement*, ed. Bryant, S., Morris, M., & Walker, J. S. F. (Greater Manchester Archaeological Unit. 1985 pp. 141-143)

Walker, J., The Role of the Frontier Settlement at Manchester in *Roman Manchester. A Frontier Settlement*, ed. Bryant, S., Morris, M., & Walker, J. S. F. (Greater Manchester Archaeological Unit. 1985 pp. 167-181)

Chapter 2

Barratt, J., *The Siege of Manchester 1642* (Bristol: Stuart Press, 1993)

Bennett, M., The Making of a Military Genius in *BBC History Magazine*, February 2017, pp. 22-27.

Civil War in Manchester and Salford, 1642 www.arthurchappell.me.uk

Dickens, S., Pre-1858 Probate and Genealogical Research. The Will of William Hallsworth, Gentleman, of Great Ancoats Street, Manchester, 1825. *The Manchester Genealogist*. Vol. 42. No. 3. 2006. pp. 239-243.

Dickens, S., *Victorian Manchester Through Time* (Stroud: Amberley. 2015)

Dore, R. N., *The Great Civil War in the Manchester Area*, 1642–46 (University of Manchester Department of Extra-Mural Studies, 1972)

English Civil War Biographies bcw-project.org

English Civil War Glossary www.historylearningsite.co.uk

English Civil War Weapons www.historyonthenet.com

Lynch, M., *The Interregnum, 1649–60* (Hodder Education: Second Revised Edition, 2002)

Oliver Cromwell www.history.com

Siege of Manchester, 1642 https://radicalmanchester.wordpress.com

Chapter 3

Bruton, F. A., *Three Accounts of Peterloo and the Story of Peterloo* (Manchester: University Press, 1921)

Corn Laws www.britainexpress.com

Dickens, S., *Victorian Manchester Through Time* (Stroud: Amberley. 2015)

Lancaster Gazette, Obituaries, 13 August 1825 p. 3.

London Gazette, Issue 15421, 24 October 1801 p. 1296.

London Times, Thursday August 19 1819.

Manchester Guardian Archive www.library.manchester.ac.uk

Manchester Guardian, Lancaster Assizes, 6 April 1822 p. 3.

Manchester Guardian, St George's Day Celebrations, 27 April 1822 p. 2.

Manchester Observer, Wednesday 11 August 1819.

Peterloo Massacre www.peterloomassacre.org

Chapter 4

A Second World War OBE and Great War DSC. Pair to Captain F. D. Struss, Merchant Navy. www.bonhams.com

Manchester Evening News, 'PALS' IN KHAKI, Friday 12 February 1915 p. 5.

Manchester Evening News, MARCH IN KHAKI. Tuesday 16 February 1915 p. 5.

Manchester Evening News, RECRUITING REVIVAL AND THEIR GOOD RESPONSE IN MANCHESTER. Wednesday 14 April 1915 p. 6.

Manchester Evening News, A NIGHT ADRIFT IN OPEN BOAT ON HEAVY SEA. HOW THE AGUILA WENT DOWN. THRILLING STORY. Wednesday 14 April 1915 p. 6.

Manchester Evening News, MANCHESTER 'PALS'. The First Casualty. Monday 29 November 1915 p. 7.

Manchester Evening News, MANCHESTER LINERS. Towed For Nine Hours Before Sinking. CREW LAND UNINJURED. Tuesday 28 March 1916 p. 4.

Manchester Evening News, PUBLIC SCHOOLS BATTALION. Friday 19 July 1918 p. 2.

Manchester Guardian, The End of the War, 5 June 1902 p. 7.

The Manchester Regiment http://regiments.org

www.traffordwardead.co.uk

www.wrecksite.eu

Chapter 5

Air Raid Precautions: April 1938–1945 www.bbc.co.uk

By Unknown http://media.iwm.org.uk

Manchester at War-Battles, Bombs and Blitz www.newmanchesterwalks.com

Manchester Blitz https://en.wikipedia.org

Manchester's Devastating Christmas Blitz www.bbc.co.uk

Manchester Evening News, LYING HUN: FICTION ABOUT MANCHESTER. Monday 22 October 1917 p. 3.

Manchester Evening News, FRANCE INVADED: TANKS PIERCE WALL. Tuesday 6 June 1944.

Manchester Evening News, Mr Churchill Announces Official Peace from Midnight: CHEERING CROWDS AND CRACKERS. Tuesday 8 May 1945.

Manchester Evening News, BANDS, DANCING, BONFIRES AND THANKSGIVING SERVICES. Wednesday, 15 August 1945.

Manchester Guardian, NIGHT RAID ON NORTH-WEST. Heavy Attack on Inland Town. MANY FIRE BOMBS. People Trapped in Shelter Rescued. 23 December 1940 p. 3.

Manchester Guardian, NIGHT RAIDERS AGAIN IN THE NORTH-WEST. 24 December 1940 p. 5.

Manchester Guardian, SUNDAY NIGHT'S BOMBARDMENT OF MANCHESTER. Casualties 'surprisingly small'- Official Statement. 24 December 1940 p. 5.

Manchester Guardian, SUNDAY NIGHT'S RAID: Attack on N.W. Town. 24 December 1940 p. 6.

Manchester Guardian, HUGE FIRES IN MANCHESTER. 24 December 1940 p 6.

The Manchester Blitz www.iwm.org.uk

The Manchester Regiment http://regiments.org

Note: Commemorative plaques are now patinated bronze, rather than coloured plaques, in a revival scheme by Manchester City Council.

ABOUT THE AUTHOR

Steven is from the Flixton area of Trafford in Manchester and is married to Sarah. They have three sons and three daughters. He is a retired charge nurse and college lecturer, with an academic background in modern history and a BA Honours degree in History from Sheffield University, an MA in Twentieth-Century History from Liverpool University and a Postgraduate Certificate in Education from Manchester Metropolitan University. His Registered General Nursing qualification was gained at Trafford General Hospital (formerly Park Hospital) in Davyhulme, Manchester, and he has twenty years of experience in nursing and teaching. He has always had an interest in local history, genealogy and archaeology, with experience of working in Roman archaeology for the Greater Manchester Archaeological Unit at Manchester University. Steven has written several journal and magazine articles on these subjects in the past, as well as writing and publishing several local history titles. He has also given talks to local history societies and schools on these subjects.

The King's Regiment is awarded the Freedom of the City of Manchester, 2010. (Photo Mamucium)

Home time: The King's Regiment, bayonets unsheathed, take to the transports after the Freedom of the City of Manchester parade, 2010. (Photo Mamucium)